Production Research

S K I L L S E T

THE INDUSTRY TRAINING ORGANISATION FOR BROADCAST, FILM & VIDEO

What are National Vocational Qualifications (NVQs/SVQs)?

The National Vocational Qualifications/Scottish Vocational Qualifications for the broadcast, film and video industry were developed by SKILLSET to create a framework for improving the standards of vocational training throughout the industry and to establish, for the first time, a framework of professional qualifications for the industry.

Standards have been developed for every occupation in the industry, to reflect the different skills and knowledge needed at different stages in a person's career. NVQs/SVQs are work-based qualifications awarded to people who can prove that they have the skills and knowledge and are able to apply them in the workplace. Because of this emphasis on workplace assessment, NVQs/SVQs are fundamentally different from other vocational or academic awards.

The standards and qualifications will be useful for employers as a guide to levels of performance for staff and freelances. They provide, for the first time, a basis for analysing job descriptions across all sectors, which is increasingly important as we rely more heavily on a freelance workforce. The standards also provide a benchmark for the design and delivery of training of employers.

Individuals will now have proof of competence and a framework for planning further development, training and progression. This will enhance their opportunities to gain employment and to move within and outside their present area of work. Individuals will also be able to judge the relevance of different training and education programmes on offer.

How do candidates achieve an NVQ?

To achieve an NVQ candidates must prove to a qualified assessor, through a formal assessment process, that they can perform competently to the standards applicable to the qualifications sought. To do so they must produce evidence of their competence for the assessor to judge. Evidence will come primarily from the assessor's observation of the candidate's performance at work, but also from a portfolio of documentary evidence compiled by the candidate. A typical portfolio might include samples and showreels, paperwork and authenticated statements from colleagues, supervisors and employers.

Who awards NVQs?

NVQs in broadcast, film and video are awarded by the Awarding Body Partnership established by SKILLSET and Open University Validation Services (OUVS). Candidates who gain NVQs will be awarded their certificate jointly by SKILLSET and the Open University.

What is SKILLSET?

SKILLSET is the national training organisation for broadcast, film, video and multimedia, and is funded and managed by the industry. SKILLSET's role is to:

'encourage the delivery of informed training provision so that the British broadcast, film, video and multimedia industry's technical, creative and economic achievements are maintained and improved.'

For further information please contact
SKILLSET
124 Horseferry Road
London SW1P 2TX

Production Research

An introduction

Kathy Chater

Focal Press

OXFORD   BOSTON   JOHANNESBURG   MELBOURNE   NEW DELHI   SINGAPORE

Focal Press
An imprint of Butterworth-Heinemann
Linacre House, Jordan Hill, Oxford OX2 8DP
225 Wildwood Avenue, Woburn, MA 01801-2041
A division of Reed Educational and Professional Publishing Ltd

℞ A member of the Reed Elsevier plc group

First published 1998

British Library Cataloguing in Publication Data
A catalogue record for this book is available from the British Library

Library of Congress Cataloguing in Publication Data
A catalogue record for this book is available from the Library of Congress

ISBN 0 240 51466 1

Printed and bound in Great Britain by
Biddles Limited, Guildford and King's Lynn

CONTENTS

INTRODUCTION

This book is based on the National/Scottish Vocational Qualification (N/SVQ) in Production Research but goes beyond the qualification in that it attempts to introduce skills needed in the industry to students and others wanting to work in production.

I've incorporated tips and examples from researchers. Getting them turned out to be more difficult than anticipated. Research is often a long and painstaking process of trying one avenue after another. As one researcher said, explaining just how a problem was solved takes pages and, unless you were working on the production, it's almost impossible to understand just why the decisions were taken because there were so many factors involved. As you will see, almost each example here illustrates more than one point about the researcher's role and much of the text consists of questions that have to be answered according to the production's needs rather than a one-size-fits-all blueprint.

There is much more to production research than just reading books, which is what most people assume when they think of research. Other factors involved include interpersonal skills, lateral thinking, the ability to work effectively and efficiently and the ability to work safely. Such aspects have not been discussed separately but are included at the points in a production where they are most important. Copyright and other legal matters also have to be taken into account at almost every stage of production so these have been discussed in separate sections to avoid repetition in the text.

ACKNOWLEDGEMENTS

The SKILLSET qualification was developed by individuals from a wide range of backgrounds, with different experiences and specialisms. The group included people from radio because, although methods of presentation are different between the visual and aural media, many of the skills, like finding information, contributors and illustrative material, are the same. The Production Research Group consisted of:

Lois Acton	Carlton Television
Peter Bailey	Freelance
Damien Chalaud	Freelance
Kathy Chater	BBC
Andrea Collett	BBC
Fiona Dodd	ITN
Jan Elson	BBC
Wayne Garvie	Granada Television
Antoinette Graves	Freelance
Debbie Gaunt	Kilroy Productions
Stephen Kelly	Freelance
Lindsay MacRae	Freelance
Geoff Prout	BBC
Maurice Raine	Freelance

Like all researchers, I have drawn heavily on the expertise of others. As well as those who have provided examples of the kinds of problems encountered while doing research, I have been helped by various trade organisations and individuals. I am grateful to David Hudson for pointing out errors in the section on copyright and to Tom Beesley and Gill Moore for helping with the section on the law – but any inaccuracies that have slipped through are my responsibility. Numerous other people and organisations, like the Association of British Photographers, FOCAL (the trade association for film libraries and researchers), the Moving Image Society – BKSTS, the MCPS, the RSPCA, the Society of Authors and the technical instructors in the BBC's Television Training Department have

patiently answered questions, generously sent printed information and generally made the task of writing this book much easier than it might have been. One of the joys of research is that you never stop learning, either by being given advice directly or by watching others work, so I'd like to thank the many other people who helped me on the way.

Kathy Chater

1

THE PRODUCTION PROCESS

What always surprises people when they first come into contact with a production, either because they get a job there or because they are appearing on a programme, is the number of people involved and how interdependent their work is. Writers for print, either books or periodicals, can closet themselves with their word processors for much of their working time, but someone employed on a film or television programme has to

work with and depend on the actions and skills of a number of people. Radio can be a more isolated occupation: a pre-recorded and edited documentary may be made by one person and a tape recorder, although live programmes require more staff. Even here, however, fewer people are needed than in film or television because radio technology is simpler.

Programmes have to be originated, developed, recorded, edited and transmitted or, in the case of non-broadcast productions, delivered to the client. Who comes up with the idea, does the development, the recording and the editing, and what part they play in the transmission or delivery is again a matter of what kind of production it is and how its day-to-day schedule is organised. Job titles are different according to the type of production and the company. The newsreader, or newscaster, or anchorman/woman, plays the same role of linking items as the presenter of a magazine programme or the host of a quiz show. Their function is the same yet what they are called varies. There are subtle distinctions between a reporter and a correspondent: reporters cover news stories generally, a correspondent has a particular area of expertise, e.g. education, the environment. The audience, however, simply sees or hears someone describing a situation.

As anyone who reads the credits on productions will know, there are a bewildering number of job titles. When SKILLSET started out to map the industry, it came up with a list of almost four hundred. It is more helpful to think of those involved in a production not as a list of jobs, but as a series of functions. This is how N/SVQs were developed by SKILLSET. The stages in a production and the job titles most often associated with them can be broken down as follows:

- Originating – coming up with the idea and doing enough research to establish its viability. This may be done by a producer, a director or a researcher.
- Selling the idea to someone. Alternatively, a gap in the market might be identified, from which a production is commissioned. In the case of complete programmes, this is usually the producer's role but on established programmes and strands, researchers may be expected to submit their ideas to an editor or producer.
- Developing the idea further – gathering information, selecting contributors, finding illustrative material such as stills, archive footage or sound, and deciding how

best to put these together. This is the central function of research and, as indicated earlier, may be done by almost any member of the production team, including production/broadcast assistants and secretaries.

- Managing the production process – getting and spending money, keeping track of it and scheduling the stages of production. The producer, production/unit manager, production co-ordinator and production assistant are the people most involved here but researchers may also be involved with negotiating fees and contracts for contributors and archive material, as well as organising and scheduling simple recordings.

- Recording. The number and nature of the people involved here will depend on whether the production is recorded in the studio or as an OB (outside broadcast), either live or for later transmission, or using a single camera on location. Director, production assistant, camera operator, camera assistant and sound recordist are the job titles used here. For multi-camera recordings, there will also be vision mixers, technical managers, floor/stage managers, assistant floor/stage managers, lighting directors and a host of other people handling the technical aspects. In these days of multi-skilling, it's also worth noting that some of the roles on a portable single camera (PSC) recording on location may double up. Directors might operate the camera or record the sound. There may be no production assistant: the researcher might carry out the function of listing the shots or this may be done later in the office from the rushes.

- Editing, including writing any commentary needed. This is usually done by the director and picture editor but researchers may supervise the simpler sequences. In news and current affairs, journalists write their own scripts. On training and promotional videos, a specialist writer may be employed.

- Dubbing. The process of balancing and adding any additional sound needed is carried out by a specialist, supervised by the director/production assistant/researcher, depending on the complexity of the work required.

- Publicising the programme may involve the whole

production team or may be carried out by a specialist department within the broadcasting organisation for which it is made. Alternatively, the arrangement of the press launch and publicity generally may be handed over to a PR company.

- Transmitting the programme or delivering it in the case of, for example, a training video which is not broadcast. A lot of documentation is involved in transmission which is usually done by the producer/director and production assistant.

To this list, some might add justifying the production and finding scapegoats when the reaction is less than adulatory. These are the stages that every production goes through, whether it is done in a few hours for a news bulletin or over a year for a special programme to celebrate an important event.

Media studies courses lay emphasis on audience research and this is, indeed, of great importance to management, especially those involved in scheduling programmes. However, those actually making the programme do not normally carry out audience research or test public interest in an idea or new format. Production staff must, of course, have a clear idea of their audience but do not undertake these tasks, which are handed over to specialist companies. Programme-makers tend to personalise the audience, seeing the production as being made for people like their younger sister or their Uncle Joe.

Production research is the process of finding the elements from which a production is made up: primarily information and contributors but also additional material like archive footage, sound and still pictures. The work involved, whether it's checking questions for a quiz show, finding celebrities for a daytime magazine programme or getting archive material, varies according to the kind of programme. Often the research does not stop when the programme is completed: there may be accompanying material, like fact sheets, to be written and publicity to be arranged. Who does it alters according to the type and scale of the production and the number of people in the team.

Researchers also have to be able to use their skills across more than one type of programme, although inevitably they will find that they are better suited to some areas than others. The abilities needed for factual programmes, like news and documentaries or educational productions, where the conveying

of information is paramount, are different from those employed in light entertainment programmes.

In broadcasting and non-broadcast video-making, there is a great deal more to do than simply find material: the implications of how it is to be used, the legal constraints involved and a host of other considerations have to be taken into account. Each programme will present different problems to which different answers must be found. This book, therefore, outlines the possibilities to be considered when undertaking research and the kind of questions that need to be asked at each stage of the production process. Every programme is different and there is no one, right answer to each situation.

Not every programme will have a researcher. Producers or directors may do their own research, assisted by the production assistant or the secretary. Some researchers, however, will be expected to schedule shoots and direct interviews and simple sequences. Some productions will have a single researcher; others will have more than one, especially where specialist skills like archive film research are involved. In news and current affairs, journalists, reporters and correspondents will do research as well as write scripts and present pieces to camera. Research does not end with the first day of recording. Although the greater and most important part of the work should be done by then, the process continues sometimes until after transmission. This particularly applies if a book tied to the production is to be published, or the programme is asking for contributions from the audience, e.g. *Crimewatch* or *Crimestoppers*.

Whatever the job title, the process of research covers more than the skills of finding the raw material of a production. Programme making demands other, personal, attributes. Working as part of a team, negotiating skills, ways of making suggestions, anticipating and solving problems all depend on knowing how a programme is put together (including how much it will cost) and what contribution each member of the production team makes.

Types of production

The process of classifying productions can be done in a number of ways. There's probably a good dinner-party game or a PhD thesis to be made out of it. Is it a sitcom drama or light

entertainment? Is *Have I Got News For You* a quiz show, a news programme or satire? Where does the *Jimmy Young Show* fit in?

The audience would broadly distinguish between drama and factual programmes. People working in directing and in the technical areas of the industry would probably make a division between live and pre-recorded productions and studio-based, multi-camera work; between outside broadcasts (like a sporting event) and single-camera location shoots on film or video. Picture editors distinguish between productions shot on film (which are now almost always dramas) and those on video, although film editors are increasingly cross-trained to use video.

There are no very clear divisions for researchers, but probably the major distinction is the type of audience: are they watching to be informed or to be entertained? Researchers tend to gravitate towards factual programmes or to entertainment but here, too, there are overlaps: a popular science programme might use the format and techniques of a studio games show, for example. Holiday programmes both inform and entertain.

Working as part of a team

Management gurus have written many books about team-work. They have described techniques for keeping people productive, for negotiating. There are other books on communication and interpersonal skills. You can read these books – any bookshop or library will have a large number – but what they boil down to, whether the team is three or three hundred people, is:

- *There's nowt so queer as folk.* You have to know the foibles and characters of the people you work with. If you have a director or producer who dithers, knowing when and how to apply pressure to get an essential decision made can only be done if you understand that person.

- *You do your job, I'll do mine.* This involves knowing what other team members do and what their responsibilities on this particular production are. In a small, independent company, it may be the researcher's job to negotiate and issue contracts to contributors or to clear the rights to use archive material, or it may be the

production assistant's. In a large company, there may be a contracts assistant or even a whole department to deal with these matters. You have to know whose responsibility it is – don't assume these things happen.

- *Do you want it Thursday or do you want it good?* Anticipating the implications of your work for other people is essential. If a complicated graphics sequence is required, you need to have an idea of how long it will take, which mainly comes from experience or simply asking. You also need to know what other work the graphics designer is doing in order to decide when you have to give the information needed and how to explain the requirements. You must be aware of deadlines and what can be achieved within them. If you have only enough time to put together the bare outline of a situation, you need to decide what is essential and what else can be added if time and resources permit.

- *Show me yours and I'll show you mine.* Negotiating. This might be called the art of making the greatest number of people the least unhappy. Inevitably, people will see the production differently. You may think that a contributor you have found is essential to the production, but the director or producer disagrees and would prefer someone else, someone you consider weaker. Techniques to get your view accepted range from throwing a mega-tantrum to laying out your arguments patiently and logically to nagging gently for weeks on end: which you choose depends on who you are dealing with and how convinced you are of the validity of your position.

Sometimes you get asked for some really stupid things. I was working on a children's programme when one of the presenters asked for 'real film of pirates'. Film has only been around for a hundred years, so there's no point in wasting time trying to find film of Blackbeard or any other seventeenth-century villain. There won't be any photographs of them either: the first ones were done in 1837.

Maurice Raine, freelance film researcher

Compromises always have to be made: often this is a matter of expense, but it may be that what is envisaged is not technically possible. Reasons have to be explained tactfully. Often something genuinely is impossible but the ability to analyse a problem and think laterally is useful here. Always try to offer an alternative rather than saying a flat 'can't do'.

2

DEVELOPING, RESEARCHING AND PRESENTING IDEAS

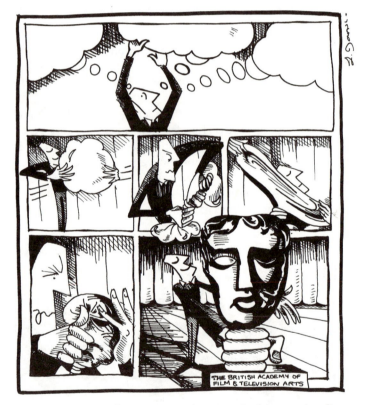

THE BRITISH ACADEMY OF FILM & TELEVISION ARTS

Hours and hours of programme time on television and radio have to be filled every day, month and year. The days when the BBC could say, 'There is no news tonight' and move smartly on to the next programme have gone. The increase in the number of broadcasting channels and radio stations means that an enormous quantity of ideas is needed, not only for whole

programmes but for individual items within magazine programmes. There is also a large market for training, promotional and corporate videos, most of which are commissioned, but organisations may be open to suggestions if a gap in the market can be identified.

Example

My work involves making medical videos. Some are for training purposes: for our staff, on a technique, about good practice or educational films for students. We also make patient information films: what to expect from a particular operation, feeding babies, that sort of thing.

People come to me with ideas and the money to make the videos comes from two sources:

1. Sponsorship from a drug company or an equipment manufacturer. We retain editorial control but they get a credit and a copy of the video which they can use for goodwill purposes.
2. From our own funding, if I identify a gap in the market, like our video on how to break bad news. I did a bit of research in film libraries and found that all the films on the subject were either not very good or out of date. I asked round and found that there was tremendous interest because there wasn't much on the subject. It made five times its cost.

David Cleverly, Producer, Video Unit
St George's NHS Healthcare Trust and Medical School

Ideas

Desperate for ideas? Think quickly of any three subjects, for example religion, geography and drama. Find a common link. Why do people in different countries react so strongly to religious portrayals in films and theatre? Examples could be the reactions to Martin Scorsese's film *The Last Temptation of Christ*, Jimmy McGovern's television film *Priest* and the documentary *Death of a Princess*.

Or language, architecture and women. Do men and women's tastes in architecture differ? How, and what kind of language do they use to express any differences? Do male and female architects describe their creations differently?

Ashe Hussain, freelance producer

Every production starts with an idea. Luckily, they are everywhere. Relatively few of them are totally original. Often it is a matter of taking something that has been done before but presenting it in a novel way to try to convince the audience that this is new, relevant and exciting. This particularly applies to news and current affairs programmes: finding yet another angle on a long-running political crisis or the plight of the homeless consumes many hours in production meetings.

In documentary areas, light entertainment or children's programmes, the scope for coming up with a new idea is much wider. A programme or programme item could theoretically be made about anything. Good research comes from being alert to every possibility and from making contact with people who are likely to bring you stories. Ideas can come from:

- printed material (books, newspapers, periodicals, press releases etc.);
- conferences;
- trade fairs;
- experts and specialists, including journalists;
- other personal contacts;
- previous programmes, both radio and television.

Many ideas, especially in news and current affairs programme-making, come from an article in a newspaper or magazine, but there are other sources. The starting point may come from a conversation overheard on a bus or in a shop or from a notice delivered by the local council through the letterbox. Established programme strands and broadcasting companies receive press releases and calls from regular contacts. A letter from a viewer or a letter in the correspondence column of a newspaper might form the starting point. Work done for other productions often leads on to another programme.

> It's important to go to the archives themselves whenever you can, not just telephone. While working in a film archive on a completely different subject, I noticed they had film of Emily Davison's funeral cortege marching from Bloomsbury to Kings Cross to put the coffin on the train and also of her funeral service at Morpeth. She was the suffragette who threw herself at the King's horse at the Derby in 1913. I suggested this as an idea for a programme, which was made.
>
> *Maurice Raine, film researcher*

Ideas also need a peg on which to hang them – why should this particular idea be done now? With general, news-oriented programmes, it is not enough that something is topical, or even simply interesting, the questions to be asked are how many will this affect, why should several million people care?

For more specialist programmes, there might be a different peg. A book might be about to be published or a survey produced. Anniversaries of an event are an old favourite, but it will need to be a significant anniversary – twenty-seven years is not significant, twenty-five or thirty is. A case for the importance of the event will also have to be made. It may be a hundred years since the invention of a gadget but unless that object changed the world in some respect, the response will be 'so what'? Even though the audience may be smaller here, you are still thinking in hundreds of thousands.

Turning the idea into a programme

So you have a good idea: it may either have been your own or have been given to you by a producer or editor. It is not yet, however, a programme or programme item worth watching. All ideas need to be translated from the medium in which they originated into a format for a particular kind of production and audience.

First, the ways in which the idea can be presented must be considered. These will depend partly on the medium: television, radio or non-broadcast productions, like a training video. Things can be done on television that can't be done on radio because they need to be seen. Conversely, it is very easy to make a television programme that is simply radio with pictures: the viewer misses nothing if de-fleaing the cat while it's on. Non-broadcast productions, especially training videos, usually have a much higher level of dedication in their audience so they will often settle for less demanding, and less expensive, methods of presentation.

Next consideration is the programme format: is it studio-based or recorded on location, either as a portable single camera (PSC) production or as an outside broadcast (OB)? Is it recorded on film, videotape or audio tape? Is a presenter or a reporter used or not? Is it to be broadcast live or pre-recorded? All these will affect how the idea can be developed.

> I've shot the same film twice. We made a video on coping with bereavement for two markets. One version was for social workers where we used a house as the location and the other, for doctors and nurses, was shot in a hospital with people in uniforms. I used very similar scripts.
>
> *David Cleverly, Producer, Video Unit*
> *St George's NHS Healthcare Trust and Medical School*

Information can be presented in a number of ways. Not all will be appropriate to both television and radio or to a particular programme format (studio-based, outside broadcast, single camera productions recorded on location), but they include the following:

Narrative methods:
- in-vision presenter/reporter;
- out-of-vision commentary;
- unscripted fly-on-the-wall;
- dramatisation/reconstruction.

Using contributors:
- talking heads;
- group discussions;
- phone-ins;
- show with a studio audience, who may take part in some way.

Visual methods:
- specially recorded film/video;
- graphics/animation;
- demonstrations using props and/or models;
- archive footage;
- still pictures.

Aural methods (which can be specially recorded or archive):
- music;
- sound effects;
- spoken word.

In the last few years there have been two programmes on the separation of conjoined twins, one made by Jon Palfreman and shown in the *Horizon* strand which emphasised the medical

aspects, and the other made by Mark Galloway at Yorkshire Television for *Network First* which concentrated on the human angle. Although the subject was the same, the productions used different methods to tell their stories. A breakdown of the sequences in each is shown on pp 16–17.

Which channel is the programme to be shown on? Who is the audience? Is it for a mass audience who know little about the subject or for a more specialised segment of the population who can be expected to bring more knowledge to it? How old are the majority of the viewers likely to be? What kind of social/ educational/ethnic background is it aimed at?

It is also essential to be aware of the programme's budget: the most brilliant idea in the world is useless to the programme if there isn't the money to do it. You must be aware of the cost of film crews, editing, special effects and graphics, not only in money but also in time. If the programme is going out next week and the special effects you think essential will take three days to film and five days in post-production, forget it or think again of a cheaper, faster way to achieve a similar effect. You don't always need to fly to India to do a programme about Indian customs. It may be something you could record in London or Bradford – less fun to do, admittedly, but you'll have a better chance of getting your idea made.

Selling an idea

> Watch television all the time.
> *Dee Dee Glass, independent producer*

Those working regularly for a programme or company quickly learn the type of subject the editor or producer is interested in and how to persuade them to do the idea. It may, however, have to be presented to an unknown person in order to get a commission. As well as doing enough preliminary research to establish that the production is worth doing, you will need to do some research on the people to whom it is being sold. Some broadcasters issue information about the kind of programme they are looking for and some hold meetings. You can always ring people who are likely to commission ideas and ask them what they want but you also need to watch the kind of programmes they produce to decide both if your idea

is one likely to attract them and how it should be treated. BAFTA (the British Association of Film and Television Arts) also hosts discussions and presentations about the kinds of productions companies are looking for.

As the following example shows, selling a complete production, as opposed to an item for a magazine programme, is largely the responsibility of the producer and those involved in the management of the production rather than a researcher. The researcher, however, may be involved in preparing the presentation and doing research for it.

When Tottenham police set up their Domestic Violence Unit, the first of its kind, I decided there were three possible commissioners who'd be interested:

1. John Willis at *First Tuesday*;
2. Roger Bolton at Thames TV;
3. Paul Hamann at *Inside Story*.

I made a slightly different approach to each. John Willis's previous work suggested he'd respond to a revelatory approach, Roger Bolton to a more journalistic one and Paul Hamann to an observational, fly-on-the-wall film. I emphasised those ways of doing the story to each. 'Partners in Crime' was eventually made for *Inside Story* in 1988 and transmitted in 1989 on BBC-1.

Dee Dee Glass, independent producer

(The successful treatment is shown on pp 20–22.)

Although commissioners usually say they only want one side of A4, an indication of the type of audience it is aimed at and the cost of the production, this example shows that 'rules' are sometimes there to be broken.

If the idea has been sent to the right people and presented in a way that attracts them, the next stage is usually a meeting. You need to prepare for this carefully. Is the meeting to be formal or informal? Who is the presentation being made to? What are their known interests? What is their level of knowledge? What are the key points that need to be got across? How are contributors to be used: are they there to give their opinion, to illustrate by their experience or because they have some particular skill to demonstrate? What benefits will the commissioner get from the production? What kind

Horizon

Opening sequence: Arrival in Philadelphia of conjoined twins Dao and Duan from an orphanage in Bangkok, and them settling into the home of a nurse and her doctor husband who are looking after them while they are in America.

Section 2: The first visit to the hospital in Philadelphia where the separation is to take place. A voice-over explains the background and a doctor describes the cause of conjoined twins. A graphics sequence provides illustration.

Section 3: Alternation of the twins' visits to hospital to have tests done to explore their physical condition and their life in their new home, including a birthday party. This section makes much use of X-rays taken by the medical team and animation showing the twins' internal structure. There is also a brief explanation of how conjoined twins were given the name 'Siamese', illustrated with photographs of Chang and Eng Bunker, the first celebrity conjoined twins who, like Dao and Duan, came from Thailand to America.

Network First

Opening sequence: The parents of Katie and Eilish talking about their reactions to the birth of their Siamese twins (the word Siamese is employed rather than the medical term, conjoined).

Section 2: The twins in their home and the small village outside Dublin where they live and are known. A brief voice-over explains the cause of conjoined twins. A doctor (in his office) talks about the pros and cons of separation and the twins' mother talks about the problems caused by their physical condition and their personalities.

Section 3: This is concerned with the question of separation. A doctor explains to camera the medical problems and the parents talk about their reservations. The parents travel to Great Ormond Street Hospital in London to meet twins separated five years ago and their parents. After a second visit to Great Ormond Street and a discussion with a surgeon there, the decision to go ahead is made.

Section 4: The first operation is shown and then the period of recovery after skin expanders have been inserted to facilitate reconstruction after the separation. An explanation of what was done and why is given by a voice-over and surgeons. The twins' temporary carer, Barbara Headley, describes their psychological reactions.

Section 4: A surgeon briefly describes in a piece to camera the decisions to be made about how the separation is to be carried out. The twins are seen after the first operation (not filmed) while the position and purpose of the skin expanders inserted are explained to their mother by a doctor. The parents describe how the twins are coping with recovering from the first operation both physically and mentally.

Section 5: The planning meeting for the main operation and the operation itself, illustrated with X-rays and animation sequences. The operation is shown in detail with explanations of what is being done by the surgeons while they work.

Section 5: A brief sequence of the planning meeting for the main operation. A doctor summarises in a piece to camera.

Section 6: The recovery period in the hospital and at home. The temporary parents (who have decided to adopt) talk about the psychological effects of the separation. The twins' current situation and their future prospects are described. The programme concludes with the twins' fourth birthday party, held at the hospital, and the chief surgeon describing his feelings about the operation's success.

Section 6: Eilish is shown alone after the operation (not filmed). A brief voice-over explains that Katie died a few days after the operation from heart failure. The parents talk about Eilish's reactions, about their feelings and emphasise that they feel they made the right decision.

of audience is it aimed at? What are the possible methods of realisation? How much are the programme elements likely to cost? What deadlines need to be met? Are there likely to be any logistical difficulties and, if so, what alternatives are there? What copyright, legal and ethical considerations need to be taken into account? Is any further information needed?

Get the meeting worked out in your mind, prepare answers to what their problems are likely to be. You're selling yourself as much as your idea. Interrogate your idea, find all the weak points to make sure you've got them plugged. Don't go in mob-handed, take a maximum of one other person with you. Be prepared to listen but make the points you want to. If you don't know the answer to something, don't bullshit, say you'll need time to think and will get back to them. Don't give them an opportunity to say no.

Dee Dee Glass, independent producer

The basic ideas or treatment can be illustrated with selected press cuttings, stills and film clips. Formal presentations, usually to managerial level commissioners in the area of non-broadcast productions, will probably focus less on the content of the programme than on the audience and the cost. The methods mentioned before can be used, perhaps with the addition of overheads, slides and flip charts.

Treatments

You may also be involved in writing a treatment, which is an expanded version of the brief giving more detail about how the idea is to be realised. This may also include the target audience and potential costs.

Treatments are prepared to sell a programme idea. Commissioners may have a set format for presentation but whatever other information they require, the programme must be summarised in a sentence or two in a way that will persuade the audience to watch it, including what's called in the advertising world the USP – unique selling point. What does this programme have that no other does? The short description

in the programme listings published by magazines and newspapers is the kind of thing that's needed.

Some programmes, like gardening programmes, have a regular and devoted following. The makers know they can rely on a core audience so they tend not to go overboard with a description of the programme's contents. It's enough to say that new potting techniques, a visit to a particular garden or planning a border is included. The core audience will tune in whatever and others, who have some interest in one of the subjects, perhaps because they have just acquired a garden, will also watch but their numbers will be small.

Current affairs programmes need to draw in a much larger proportion of the potential audience for each edition and must fight for their viewers, so need to emphasise the importance of what they are showing. Radio listeners are inclined to leave the same station on all day. Much less space is allocated to radio programmes in listings in newspapers or periodicals. They must rely on the publicity value that links with news stories or anniversaries will bring to attract an addition to their usual audience.

Next in the treatment comes a longer description of the content of the production and how the various elements will be presented: specially shot footage, archive material, interviews etc. Expand on the USP. Does the programme have access to a particular place or event, does it include people of particular interest, either because they are celebrities or because they have something of great interest to say? Does the programme contain information that radically changes the accepted view of a situation?

The answers to these questions will influence which people and organisations to approach for information, who will be needed as contributors and where the recording will take place. Once a treatment has been accepted, however, it is not set in stone. It is not a one-off decision made at the beginning of the production but will change as research in greater depth is done, and you must be alert to this during the whole production process. If one method turns out to be impossible or inappropriate, others must be considered, so the development of an idea and the way in which it is presented will last throughout the production process.

'Cagney and Lacey in Tottenham' (became 'Partners in Crime')

WPS Colette___ has been in the Met for nearly six years. A graduate of Warwick University, she thought that being a policewoman would give meaning to her life. WPC Annette___ joined the force nine years ago. She is older and seemingly less ambitious than Colette – though this may have something to do with Annette's husband being an oft-unpromoted PC on the Wembley drug squad. The two met on vice duty in Stoke Newington. Therein lie the roots of their current jobs.

Colette and Annette speak glowingly of the hookers they met on vice. Their contempt is reserved for kerb-crawlers and pimps. The two women say that their daily exposure to the unchecked male violence in the women's lives combined with the routinely ignored status that domestic violence held in general police work, made them realise how necessary it was to have facilities to deal with the victims of domestic violence on a wider basis than grudgingly enforcing the law. In July 1987, Annette and Colette began such a programme within the Tottenham Community Policing Unit. In the first five months, they dealt with 319 cases. During January and February 1988, 174 new ones came in. And in March 1988 alone, Annette and Colette had over 100 new cases.

Saddled with the grand title of Domestic Violence Unit, the two women presently share a minute, two-desk office with their male boss, Inspector___. In addition to their duties with domestic violence, Annette and Colette are expected to deal with mental health in the community, neighbourhood watch, self-defence training and Broadwater Farm (which they both claim they have never felt unsafe walking around and which they say is one of the most law-abiding parts of their patch). They both freely admit that they spend virtually no time on any of their duties other than domestic violence. Considering that the volume of work in that area alone could easily occupy half a dozen officers, it hardly seems surprising that they have neither the time nor the inclination to do any other.

Colette and Annette nominally work a forty-hour week – either 9 to 5 or 10 till 6. They do not go on call-outs, but concentrate on following up every reported case of domestic violence. They are often quite clever in inventing ways to make contact with women – especially

if the man is not in custody. Annette once pretended to be selling Tupperware. In practice, they find that weekends are good for taking long and difficult statements and that crucial community and women's group meetings often take place at night.

Since their job extends from statement-taking in the station and counselling in Wimpy Bars to liaising with social services, DHSS, housing departments and medical services, as well as a wide range of diplomatic and occasionally extra-legal activities on behalf of women trying to remove either their belongings or the men involved permanently from a jointly occupied home, their hours are nearly as unpredictable as the job itself.

Unlike virtually all other members of the Met, Annette and Colette have won over a wide range of community groups and are the only police unit positively encouraged by Haringey Council. This is undoubtedly due to their unorthodox methods as well as their outspoken condemnation of male violence. They see the most important and inviolable part of their job as being there to support the victim (99 per cent of the time a woman). If the alleged assailant is in cells when they arrive at work, Annette and Colette never see him. They feel that this is the male police officers' job. They will help women break into their homes, and will arrange for locks to be changed, council property to be put in the woman's name, solicitors, medical and other evidence leading to injunctions and, of course, places of safety at refuges (a variety for Afro-Caribbean, Asian and white women). Annette and Colette make every woman feel like they are there only for her and that she can call on the police at any time and an instant response will be forthcoming. Inevitably this kind of impossible dependence creation needs to be examined. There is a sense that by throwing themselves so totally into their work that they are somehow making their own emotional sacrifice and therefore compensating each woman for the wrong Annette and Colette feel so acutely has been done to her.

It would be enough of a reason to film them if Colette and Annette were just attractive, articulate police officers dealing with a difficult and complex area that the police traditionally would like to ignore. However, that is only half the story. The other half is their own lives and how they accommodate their seemingly pure 'Stalker'-type view of police work with the undoubted reality of

working in the Met in Tottenham.

Colette was engaged to a PC for five years. After that relationship broke up, she swore she'd never get involved with another cop again. When she met her current boyfriend at a party, neither knew that the other was a police officer. He is a PC in Essex. She claims that her being of a higher rank matters to neither of them, but that he gets teased about it a lot. They have just bought a house and are moving in soon. They have had to apply for permission to live together, as police living in sin is frowned upon.

Neither Colette nor Annette have children. They say that some days their work makes them feel such hatred towards all men that inevitably they take it out on the ones with whom they live. They are rather more circumspect about how they cope with the violence of male police officers (both towards people generally and towards the women with whom they live), though it is obvious in observing the interactions between the two women and their male colleagues that all is not sweetness and light.

Colette and Annette's caseload does not behave like conventional police work. Apart from the fact that following up one incident may involve numerous disparate and unpredictable activities over a period of weeks, there is a high rate of recidivism. Filming them, therefore, will to a certain extent depend on a predetermination about the eventual length of the finished product: sixty minutes, ninety minutes or a series. However, given the intimate, observational nature of 'Cagney and Lacey in Tottenham', some time will need to be spent by the whole crew (which should, in any case, be as small as possible) to acclimatise everyone to filming. What would be filmed whatever the overall running time would be: initial call-outs, probably at weekends or at night, without Annette and Colette; as wide a variety as possible of following through of their cases; their homes and social lives; their relationships with other officers; the relentlessness of the emotional pressure of doing the job, day in, day out.

'Cagney and Lacey in Tottenham' is, finally, about two policewomen and how they reconcile their passion for the cause of battered women with the contradictions of their own lives as cops.

Clarifying and confirming the research brief

Once an idea or a proposal is accepted and the possible methods of realising it are decided, the research goes ahead. If you didn't originate the idea, but are the researcher on a production, you need to confirm what research will need to be done with the producer or editor. What is the aspect that is to be given most prominence and how will that be done? Who are the individuals or the kinds of people who will need to be contacted? Are there any potential problems?

> When producers are giving you instructions, be ready to write down any numbers etc. – it's irritating (and could delay the production) for busy producers to have to wait for you or repeat information.
>
> *Antoinette Graves, freelance researcher*

The essential quality of a researcher is adaptability, both to people and situations. The ability to assimilate very quickly the aims and nature of the programme being worked on, and to be able to anticipate and assess the implications and discuss them tactfully with the other people involved in the production team are major attributes.

It's easy to go away from a discussion with a very clear concept of the programme, only to find out after a considerable amount of work has been done that the producer saw it differently all along. Initially, you will need to ensure that everyone involved has the same view of how the story is to be developed. This may be done either in a production meeting with the rest of the team or one-to-one but the process of clarification is the same and depends both on listening to what the other person is saying and ensuring that you are explaining yourself clearly. Summarise and feed back to people what you have understood: 'So you think we need to…?', 'So you feel this is a story about…?', 'I see this as…is this right?'

This is easier with some people than others. There are those who like everything to be very clear-cut from the beginning but others may feel cornered and resent having to commit themselves early on. Some have firm ideas about how the story should be done while others are open to suggestions. You need to be aware of the personal preferences of those

you work with and how to choose your moment to get down to detail. Even the level of detail will vary from person to person.

Other aspects will have to be clarified with other members of the production team. There may be time already booked for doing any graphics or rostrum camera work, the recording days may already have been decided and you must know about them. This may affect which parts of your research you do first: although ordinarily information and contributors would be sought first, if time to transfer archive film has been set aside early on, efforts will need to be concentrated here initially. Whether this is done in writing or, as is much more common, verbally you will need to summarise what has been agreed and note any constraints of time or money.

All these variables mean that all those doing research must be able to think quickly on their feet. No matter what has been planned, events can change either in response to technical problems or a development in the programme treatment.

In the run-up to some European elections, I was working on a programme taking a group of people from Bolton to their twin town, Le Mans in France. The producer wanted to go to the Renault factory. We arrived just before midday. I was with another researcher and we had a bit of a problem parking. We got a puncture and while we were mending it, the factory gates opened and hundreds of Renault workers streamed out and went past us to their canteen. The sight of them gave the producer a brilliant idea.

'Let's interview some of the workers,' he said. 'Find me half a dozen who speak English – I want some vox pops.'

We pointed out that these were factory hands; they'd be about as likely to speak English as the average English worker would be to speak French but it cut no ice – he'd decided this was what he wanted. So the other researcher and I went into the canteen and no, we couldn't find anyone who spoke English. We were beginning to despair when we heard a message go out on the tannoy. So we got a request put out for anyone who spoke English to report to reception. Enough people did turn up there to give the producer the vox pops he wanted.

Stephen Kelly, ex-Granada researcher

Read, talk, experience

There are three stages of research. The first and cheapest is to speed read everything you can, either press cuttings or books, as background to the subject. From this, you decide which areas have not been covered or are worth following up in more detail. This can mean further, less superficial, reading but at some point you will have to start talking to people, which involves more trouble and expense to narrow down which ones are likely to produce what you want. Lastly, you will probably have to get out and experience the aspects that seem most promising: this can vary from simply meeting potential contributors and looking at locations to trying out activities. Which ones you decide to experience – religious cult meetings, training sessions, sky-diving – and how far you go will depend on your own abilities and your sense of self-preservation.

Identifying and approaching sources of information

Note that this section does not refer to 'facts'. As anyone who has ever listened to a politician on shaky ground protest, 'But the fact is…' will know, there are very few indisputable facts and a great number of people in academia and the media make a living out of contesting the accepted interpretation of events.

Broadly speaking, a fact is something that is capable of corroboration by external evidence. An opinion is an extrapolation from known facts. A commonly agreed 'fact' is that the population of the United Kingdom is just over fifty-eight and a quarter million people, based on census returns. A recent survey, however, found evidence of under-recording in the 1991 census. How much under-recording is a matter of opinion. It was estimated to be about one million but this cannot be proved. A fact is only a fact until someone comes up with a better alternative. Programmes can be made either by summarising the accepted facts of a situation or disputing them.

An adequate researcher will find out only what he/she is asked to. A good researcher will find out what the producer didn't know he/she wanted, and will actively look for the opposite point of view, for a range of sources who are likely to have different experiences or axes to grind.

The more sources you have access to, the more quickly this can be achieved. Your own contact book is your most valuable asset. Addresses and phone numbers in it will come from programmes you have worked on and in certain areas of programme-making you will find yourself using the same ones over and over again. However, you need to actively look for new people; audiences get very bored with finding the same old Rent-A-Quote trotted out each time a certain subject is raised.

> Always carry paper and pen because you never know when someone could give you a useful phone number or idea.
>
> *Antoinette Graves, freelance researcher*

You can increase your own list of contacts by collecting them in advance rather than waiting until you are working on a programme to start looking for them. If you keep a few index cards or a small notebook (which don't take up much room) about your person, you can quickly note any potentially useful organisations from, for example, newspaper articles or job advertisements. List the address, telephone number, fax and e-mail (if any) along with a brief note, if it's not obvious from the name of the organisation what it does. If you aren't on the Internet yourself, either at home or in the office, it's worth keeping a separate notebook of web sites.

Newspapers or periodicals will often write about a self-help group that has just been set up to support and advise some section of the population or a club catering for unusual hobbies. They are among the most difficult to contact because they are usually started by one or two people operating from their front room. In time, they may grow to a national organisation which will be listed in the telephone directory but, until then, are very hard to find in a hurry, yet can give very specific information and, equally important, contributors to a programme. The other problem with these small groups is that their organisers and addresses tend to change comparatively frequently.

While you're reading job advertisements, also note useful organisations. A charity may be advertising for an administrator or secretary – although you don't want the job, the organisation may be of use some time in the future.

Trade fairs are also a good source of contacts and addresses as well as ideas. Established programmes are usually sent press releases and a press pass to them, so if you're feeling short of ideas, and in need of some free hospitality, wander along. It is more difficult for those outside a company to learn about these events but they will be advertised in trade magazines, so if you work regularly in a particular field, e.g. science or music, look out for them in periodicals (which you should be reading anyway to keep up with your subject area).

Any change in the law will mean either the establishment of new groups to support or fight it or the abolition of organisations that are no longer relevant. There is thus a necessity to update your contacts book regularly. You also need to keep up with changes in personnel: it's not very professional to ring up asking to speak to someone who left the organisation several years ago. An occasional call to people who have been helpful in the past or organisations which have been featured in your programmes will maintain contacts and should ensure they think first of you when a story comes up – but don't overdo this, they are busy people too.

Sources of information can be broadly divided into three sections:

- Official sources, like government departments, quangos, academic schools, trades union and professional associations, self-help groups and lobbying groups. Most of these will, however, supply information with a bias towards their own interests.
- Libraries and data bases, including the Internet, which will largely gather information more indiscriminately. There are general libraries, most notably the British Library, and specialist ones which concentrate on a particular subject, e.g. the Fawcett Library which is devoted to women's history. Aslib has a directory and data base of all libraries in the country. Museums, too, are useful sources of information and experts on a particular subject as well as objects. They also divide into the general and specialist.
- Individuals with a particular area of expertise who may not be attached to an organisation; for example, freelance journalists or those whose lifelong interest has made them experts in a particular field.

The company for which you work may have a library or some arrangement with, for example, a source of press cuttings, without which no news-based programme can function efficiently. The main library in a city should also have the broadsheet newspapers on microfilm or CD-ROM, or a regional newspaper will have archives that can be used for a local story. If you or your company has access to the Internet, you will find that its resources are so vast that you get bogged down in the sheer amount of information available.

The sources listed above should be the first port of call but sooner or later their facilities will be exhausted. Where you go from there will depend very much on the nature of the research and how much time you have to do it.

If you are pushed for time, as you usually are in a news or current affairs area, you can get a broad overview of a subject or situation by contacting the relevant government department, the trade association and a self-help or lobbying group, who will each give you their view. These will differ enough to give you a story and provide the 'balance' so dear to journalists' hearts and to the broadcasting watchdogs.

Almost every area of human activity has at least one society or club and at least one periodical catering for its interests. There may also be a year-book listing companies and associations with a common purpose. Browsing through the reference section of your local library will reveal many of them. The ones you will find most useful will depend on the area in which you work but there are several directories without which few people engaged in production research can work efficiently:

- *Willings Press Guide*, which lists all the newspapers, journals and trade magazines published in this country. A separate volume covers overseas publications. If you need to read articles in specialist journals, you can find most (including some overseas publications) at the British Library Newspaper Library at Colindale in North London.
- General directories of media contacts like *Hollis Press and Public Relations Annual* or the *Media Guide*.
- Directories listing associations, societies and clubs. There are also publications covering self-help groups, campaigns and pressure groups.
- *The Charities' Digest* or the National Council for Voluntary Organisations' (NCVO) directory.

Ten tips for using the Internet

Here are ten tips for using the Internet; note that 7, 8 and 9 are relevant to all methods of research:

1. Use a subject-based search like Yahoo if you know what topic you are after. Use a searcher like Infoseek when you can be specific. Try US search engines as well. Don't confine your search to just one.

2. All search engines depend on you getting your key-words right. Take a moment with each of the engines to read the search tips which will tell you how to improve the chances that it finds what you want.

3. Especially if you are paying for your on-line time, spend a few minutes before you log on to make a list of keywords. Have a strategy mapped out. Use the thesaurus in Word on your PC to find similar words and phrases. Don't forget that US search engines need US phrases and spellings.

4. Set yourself a time limit. If after ten minutes you haven't found anything remotely resembling what you wanted, got for a walk (or log off if you're paying for the call) and think about it. Maybe you are using the wrong keyword. Maybe there is a better way to get to it, or a better engine to use. With time, you will become better at finding things quickly as you know what tools to attack the job with.

5. Use the general search engines to find some good, well-linked pages on your topic and search the links on these pages as they are likely to be more relevant.

6. You can bookmark search results to return to at a later date.

7. Resist the urge to follow links that the search throws up that look interesting but not particularly relevant. You have a specific objective when you search and you need to be disciplined.

8. Note down where you get material from, how credible the site is (is it an official site for that sort of information or not?) and note the contact e-mail or number so you can check up on things.

9. Be info-aware when you look at sites. If it isn't useful to you now, is it likely to be somewhere you want to note for the future? With experience, you will be able to judge these 'must remembers' pretty easily. They are often known as link sites – a page where someone else has already collected together all the links to one topic.

10. If you can find out information faster by looking in a book or ringing a specialist, then don't use the Internet for the sake of it.

Alexandra Barnett, freelance researcher

- Her Majesty's Stationery Office (HMSO) produces a number of publications and CD-ROMS listing sources of official information and statistics on everything from the state of the economy to bed availability in hospitals.

These cover the whole country but there are also regional publications covering a specific area. Some associations are now producing CD-ROMs of companies in their field.

Most of these publications should be available in a large company but, if you work freelance, you should consider acquiring your own copies, rather than have to trek off to a library every time you need to look something up. Reference books are, if bought new, very expensive but you can often get last year's copy from your local library, where they are sold off as new editions come out, or from charity shops. Finding last year's edition of a £90 year-book for £9 is not only a good addition to your list of potential contacts, it's also tax-deductible.

Contacting sources

Once the organisations likely to give the information needed have been identified, they must be approached. This is usually done initially over the telephone. The first contact any person or organisation usually has with a production is a telephone call. Their initial impression of the programme and its degree of professionalism will come from you, especially if you do not represent a long-established company or programme strand of which they have heard.

Anyone who is regularly asked for information over the phone has a list of personal hates at the top of which are people who don't know what they want because they haven't bothered either to find out the parameters of the subject or to think about what they need to know. They also hate people who ring up and want an enormous amount of information *right now*. This is why it is important to read as much as you can before telephoning and to prepare what you want to say, writing down all the key points you want to cover. You may have interrupted a major crisis or rung at an inconvenient time, so check that the person can talk to you now or if you should arrange another time when he/she can concentrate on what you want to know.

Establish from the outset that you are working on a production

and how the research is to be used. The extent of the help you require should be made clear and that will be the point at which any question of cost arises. People are much more money-conscious these days than they used to be – the glamour of the media may no longer be enough recompense for their time and trouble. Data bases usually make some charge and if you are accessing them through the Internet, the time you spend on-line will cost. Other bodies may have restrictions on who they will give information to for free – usually a member of their association or a subscriber to their services. If you are going to need the organisation to do some of the research for you, this must also be taken into account as they may charge for their time, depending on how much extra effort is involved.

There's a fine line, however, to be drawn between establishing whether they will give their services free and putting ideas into their heads. You may be giving them welcome publicity. Discuss whether and what kind of credit they could be given but don't commit yourself. This is where researchers can come over all humble and unimportant – say that the final word must rest with the boss.

Don't think of this stage solely in terms of getting facts and opinions. While you are talking to a source, bear in mind the other ways of presenting information. Someone from the organisation might be useful to present its views or the contact may be able to recommend someone as a contributor. The organisation might also have stills, archive footage or sound or be able to suggest a good location which will illustrate a point you are trying to put across.

Coming up against a brick wall

The initial stages of research are rather like a chain letter. You contact five people and each of them gives you some information and another three people to contact. Soon you will have more names and organisations that you can realistically talk to within your time-scale so you need to make decisions all the time about which seem the most worthwhile avenues to pursue. There will, however, come a point where one of your important sources either cannot or will not help or suggest an alternative to contact. Whether you decide to try persuasion, moral or financial, or give up and go elsewhere will depend on how essential to the programme this source is, how much time you have and how much money.

You can go back and follow up some of the names you were given before and decided not to pursue: this often works but if it doesn't, lateral thinking is the solution. What related fields are there that might provide the route back to your subject? Alternatively, the fact that you have hit a brick wall may mean that the programme is heading in the wrong direction and will need to be rethought. There may even be no story there. You may come up against a different brick wall if the story turns out to be too complicated to tell within the production's resources.

> I wouldn't pursue an idea if the expert in the field isn't prepared to give commitment to it. Some don't realise how much work is involved and they lose interest. I always make them write a very detailed outline first to see how keen they are. Nor would I go ahead if the subject is too complicated and we haven't got the facilities to handle it. A doctor came to us with an idea about a video on burns but wanted to rig up a real situation, setting up a fire in a house. That was out of our league: you have to be realistic and stay with what you're good at.
>
> *David Cleverly, Producer, Video Unit*
> *St George's NHS Healthcare Trust and Medical School*

Collecting and verifying information

While selecting the sources you contact (you could never hope to approach them all) you will have made decisions about which ones are the most authoritative, which ones represent the current view of a situation and which ones are at the moment fringe lunatics. Remember, however, that Galileo was once considered, literally, a heretic for saying that the earth went round the sun and experts said, right up to the point when it sank, that the Titanic was unsinkable. As mentioned earlier, programmes can be made either summarising accepted wisdom or presenting a completely new theory. What is your programme doing?

Most of the information turned up will suggest further avenues of research but not all can be pursued. Decisions must be made about how much information each potential source is likely to yield, how vital such information will be, how long it is

probably going to take and what it may cost. All these elements have to be balanced to produce the most effective result possible, which is not always the best that could be achieved given infinite time and resources. This is where you will have to discuss your findings and which avenues are to be further explored with the producer of the programme.

While gathering information, each source must be recorded very carefully. If it comes from published material (which may have copyright implications or require acknowledgement), you should record the title of the work, the author/s, and the date and place of publication. Adding page numbers will help you to go back to check if necessary. Publications, documents, pictures, photographs or films from specialist libraries or archives will usually have a reference number, which should also be noted.

If information comes from interviews with people, there may be restrictions on the use of information, perhaps because you have been told things off-the-record, or because anonymity has been requested. If you have taped the interview, it should be clearly marked with the name of the interviewee and the date of the interview (there's more about this in the next chapter). For certain categories of contributors, primarily actors or musicians, performance fees may be involved which you should note. Check if the budget will accommodate them.

In the initial stages, record everything. Usually what is not said is of more interest than what is. Productions are usually made to add to what is already known, even if the production is summarising the current situation. Think about the implications of the information and ask yourself 'Why is this?'. Then use the possible answers to ask questions that will give a more complete picture of the situation.

Of course the majority of people are not setting out deliberately to mislead or even lie. Some may be mistaken in what they say, so where there is a possibility of deception or error, tactful checking needs to be done. Carlton UK Television made a programme called 'A Schindler Survivor' for its series *Londoners at War*. Research was well advanced on a man named Victor Dortheimer, found with the aid of a Jewish charity, when the film *Schindler's List* opened in London.

After our production team had seen the film at a special screening, we were curious as to why neither Victor Dortheimer nor his family featured in the book or in Spielberg's film. We contacted Universal Pictures' head office in London to dig around for some basic TV research material. We were absolutely astonished to be told by their press department that there was no Victor Dortheimer – or anyone else by the name of Dortheimer, come to that – on their list of Schindler survivors. The alarm bells rang in our heads. Matthew Tombs, our researcher, was detailed to get in touch with Yad Vashem, the Holocaust museum and archive centre in Jerusalem. He asked them to check the original Schindler list held in the archives for all the 'Dortheimers' recorded on it, and fax it to us in London ASAP. Although we had no doubt that the fax would include Victor's name – along with that of his wife and sister-in-law – seeing such an official confirmation was like a legal 'seal'.

From the booklet *A Schindler Survivor: The Story Behind the Documentary* written by Ron Fisher, the producer, to accompany Carlton UK Television's programme.

When dealing with figures and tables, repeat the mantra, 'Lies, damn lies and statistics'. Surveys very rarely publish the questions asked, yet these can be of vital importance. You can get people to agree with almost anything if you phrase it in the right way. There are questions that invite the answer 'yes' and others that expect the answer to be 'no'. Inevitably, this will mean that you wind up with contradictions and discrepancies. You can go back to your sources to look for other information or ask supplementary questions. Some may not be capable of resolution. Others can be resolved but only by speculation. Be very clear about what is 'fact' and what is opinion, yours or anyone else's.

Collating, evaluating and prioritising information

If the brief has been well defined you shouldn't find it too difficult to decide what is relevant and what isn't when you come to

collect your research together. If you are working with those who are vague about what they want, you will probably need to check with them at intervals that you are working along the right lines.

Knowing when to stop is always a problem: researchers live with a nagging feeling that, given a little more time and money, they could find a single source of all information, rather than two sources and a gap; the perfect contributor rather than a choice between two who are very good; the ideal location rather than one with a few drawbacks. Deadlines or the budget will impose a halt: at some stage you will have to say 'I can live with that'.

Inevitably, much of the material will turn out to be irrelevant to the programme brief. It helps to think of the brief in terms of a question to be answered. This should help to decide what is and what isn't relevant. Does what has been found help to answer this question, or does it really apply to a different one? Extraneous material should be omitted from the final presentation – but not thrown away.

It is not uncommon to find that something that turns out to be irrelevant to the programme brief is in itself of such interest or importance that the brief may have to be re-evaluated, in which case you will have to discuss this with those who have the authority to make any changes. Methods of realisation also need consideration at this stage: some information may be difficult to present in your programme's format or within its budget.

Presenting research findings

At some stage research findings must be presented to the producer or editor, either verbally or in writing. This can be in a production meeting which the whole team attends or in an informal chat in the bar. It's also a good opportunity to discuss in more detail how the information can be treated.

The level of detail to be included will depend on the nature of the brief and on how much discussion you have already had with the other members of the team during the research process. On a long-term project, you may already have talked through most aspects but on a programme with a very short time-scale, you may have been entirely left to your own devices. Whether you are doing it verbally or in writing, summarise the

story and list the contributors, who they are and what they will say, highlighting their anecdotes or opinions and how well you think they will come across on screen. Then, depending on the other ways of presenting information which you have agreed, add details of locations, archive footage, graphics and stills which can be used for illustration, along with any problems you can foresee.

3
SELECTING AND WORKING WITH CONTRIBUTORS

While collecting information as many sources as possible in
the time scale allowed should be sought out. A great deal of
factual material will be accumulated but you are almost always
also looking for people to contribute directly to the programme

by appearing on it. Most will be interviewed but others may be there to demonstrate a skill or to give a performance of some kind, like singing or dancing.

Contributors add authenticity and human interest to a production. Broadly speaking, they should should be used for three reasons:

- Authority – an expert on a subject or the spokesperson for an organisation. He/she will offer opinions.
- Experience – a person who has first-hand knowledge of a subject or an event. He/she will relate anecdotes, or express emotion. People who are the subject of a portrait or appear on a chat show can be included in this group because it is their experiences that have made them what they are.
- Ability – someone with a skill to demonstrate. Quiz show contestants fall into this category.

For some programmes, people may be needed to represent all three categories and indeed a range of information, opinions and experiences should be represented whenever possible. News and current affairs usually have contributors from the first two categories, consisting of people who will offer contrasting opinions or experiences. If you are doing an item on the health service, for example, you might find a minister for the government's opinion on the situation, a representative from a professional association, like the British Medical Association, who could either give their official opinion or their members' experiences, and a patient who would provide experience from a different perspective.

Factually based programmes consist largely of information and contributors. In news and current affairs programmes, this is very apparent and the two are usually linked by a reporter or at least an editorial voice-over. In more purely documentary productions, the contributor(s) will be the focal point and information will be conveyed less directly: there may be no commentary or any voice-over might come from the contributor(s) recorded on a wild track. For a chat show, or an interview on a daytime magazine programme, the contributor is the whole point of the item.

While gathering information for a programme, potential contributors must also be considered. They may come from all the sources listed in the previous chapter on gathering

information and indeed may be the people from whom the information comes. This is not, however, always the case. Although information may come from a particular person in an organisation, he/she might not be the right one to be interviewed for the programme. It might be more appropriate to use someone in a position of greater authority – who may need to be briefed by the informant before the recording is made.

Contributors should not be used, however, solely to present facts directly to camera. This is visually dull, although sometimes unavoidable in news programmes when there has not been enough time to set up alternative methods. Very rarely does the viewer need to see a contributor in order to understand factual information. Radio is a slightly different case but even here facts can usually be put across more concisely in other ways. When you are selecting contributors who are going to be interviewed for the programme, look for the ones who have interesting opinions, concisely expressed, or good stories to tell. Those who can only give factual information may be helpful in giving you background material but if they have nothing beyond this, they won't be able to add anything that will illuminate the facts, which is the major point of using contributors.

Figures are a case in point. When someone, usually an MP, starts reciting statistics – 'This government has increased spending by three point five per cent in real terms and is now spending one and a half million pounds more than it was two years ago…' – the audience's eyes glaze and their fingers wander to the zapper. Graphics put statistical points across much more economically and memorably but this is a studio technique: suddenly dropping a computer-generated pie chart into the middle of a sequence recorded on location looks bizarre.

Presenting statistics on radio in an interesting way is notoriously difficult. On radio, information can usually be better presented by the use of scripted material than by an interviewee. Keep the different methods of realisation in mind when considering contributors.

Kinds of contributors

The kinds of people selected for a programme will partly depend on the subject and partly on the audience expected or

targeted. This is not to say that no-one over twenty should appear on a youth programme nor that everyone on a programme dealing with retirement should be in receipt of a pension. It is very easy to represent only one part of the population, people like you. Inevitably, you will look with more interest and approval on people who reflect aspects of your experience. When listing the sources you will approach for information and contributors, bear in mind the need to represent a spectrum of experiences and backgrounds. Consider where you will find contributors to cover the range of:

- age;
- educational background;
- social background;
- ethnic background;
- degree and nature of any disability.

As the following example shows, the story and the contributors should complement each other: the question asked was about women's rights, so the decision was made not to include men but there had to be 'a spread of ages and backgrounds'.

> At the end of 1994, I was assistant producer on *The Last Word*, a television programme where a group of women, led by Germaine Greer, discussed current issues. My job was to find subjects for them to talk about and women to take part. I read newspapers and magazines and listened to programmes for subjects. They had to be what people were thinking and talking about at the time, what we called the 'zeitgeist', and then get a particular take on it that no-one else was doing. Once we'd isolated an angle, I and the producer found women who could take part. We did something on adoption and fostering, asking 'Is it every woman's right to have a child?'. It was difficult to find subjects that hadn't been covered elsewhere and to find women from a spread of ages and backgrounds who could hold their own with Germaine Greer.
>
> *Geoff Prout, freelance assistant producer*

There are, however, other considerations. On Geoff Prout's show, they had to be women who would not be overshadowed

or overawed by Germaine Greer, which presupposes either experience of appearing in programmes or strong and confidently expressed convictions. In radio, particularly, the contributors should be chosen so their voices are distinguishable from each other but this is also a good idea in television, which means seeking out not just different tonal qualities of voice, but also accents (which may also be an indication of social background).

Stereotypes are tempting. Sometimes they are necessary, sometimes it's just laziness or shortness of time that leads to their selection. If you are doing a vox pop and finding contributors on location, stereotypes are useful: if they say what you would expect them to from their appearance, the audience will think smugly 'I knew they'd say that'. If their views do not match what the audience expects, the reaction will be one of surprise. Either way, you can't lose.

Contacting contributors

Sometimes people don't try the easiest and fastest solution to a problem because it seems too obvious. A guest, who'd been booked for a live programme the following morning, pulled out at about 5.15 p.m. I needed someone who was based in either Glasgow or London and I'd exhausted my Glasgow possibilities. I browsed through *Who's Who* – if you do this often enough, it's easy to skim read because you know what you're looking for. I wanted someone who was an established academic, perhaps had been at the London School of Economics and had written papers or books on the subject.

I tried a few people but got nowhere and was unable to track down the people they'd recommended (if someone can't do a job, always ask them if they can suggest anyone else). Then I saw the entry for Professor Kenneth Minogue. Problem: no address, no telephone number, no contact point at all. I tried the LSE and got nowhere again. So I went for the obvious (but far-fetched possibility of any success) and dialled Directory Enquiries and asked for a K. Minogue in London.

And, do you know, there was only one in London and his answering machine opens with: 'No, I'm not Kylie

> Minogue's father and I'm not related to her...'. I obviously wasn't the first person to have tracked him down this way but suspect certain reporters had wished hopefully he was Kylie's father. I left a message and within about half an hour he phoned back, said he'd do the programme and it was all fixed. He was also much better than the person who'd pulled out at 5.15 p.m.
>
> *Ashe Hussain, freelance radio producer*

Most of the time, you will contact potential contributors directly, as in the example above. There are times when you will need to go through a third party. Celebrities, for example, should be contacted through their agents; representatives of government or large organisations through the press department of their ministry or company; MPs through their political party, etc.

If you're working in a sensitive personal area, it may be preferable to involve another person, someone the potential contributor already knows and trusts, to approach him/her on your behalf. The organiser of a self-help group from whom you obtained information about, for example, cot deaths will probably be able both to suggest a member of the group who could be interviewed for the programme about his/her experience and to act as go-between. Other intermediaries might be used.

> While working on a documentary about breast cancer, I saw a story in a local newspaper about a woman who had had breast cancer. Her details seemed to be exactly right for the case study we needed. I could have found her number through local help groups or electoral registers but I decided to call the journalist who wrote the article. This was a quicker way too but it meant that the journalist could ring the lady and ask if she was willing to speak to me. I was also able to find out from the journalist how the lady felt about the media.
>
> (Warning! Journalists may get fed up with being asked to do this sort of thing but there may be a trade-off you can offer – though watch you don't give them your story before it's broadcast.)
>
> *Antoinette Graves, freelance researcher*

Journalists may also expect a fee for this – especially if they're freelance. The kind of trade-off mentioned might be to offer them a story, perhaps one of the people you have already decided not to use in your production.

As mentioned in the previous section, those you talk to will gain their impression of the production from you, but you learn a lot from the initial telephone call to potential contributors. When you do get to talk, does the person sound confident, in charge and enthusiastic about the subject? Can he/she put across views clearly and simply? Are there any good stories they can tell? Do they have any communication problems, such as a very strong accent, a speech impediment or an irritating mannerism, like saying 'Innit?' every few words? These need not preclude them from the programme – you might be doing something on speech impediments or inarticulacy – but they are factors to be taken into account.

The following example shows both the kind of criteria used to decide on interviewees for a particular programme and the importance of preparing questions to produce replies to help inform the decisions.

The production in question involved VE and VJ commemorations. I contacted a number of veterans and, after confirming their identity and explaining how I got their name and number, I checked it was a convenient time to talk and asked the following questions:

Are you planning to attend any of the commemorations in London?
This question not only established whether they might be able to pop into the studio in the veterans' centre but also helped elicit how they felt about the commemorations and the war. If they were not planning to attend, a judgement could be made as to whether expenses would be offered for the contributor to attend, depending on the nature of their contribution. The consequences of this decision might also include having to provide someone to meet the contributor with a wheelchair etc.

Which service were you in?
What campaigns were you involved with and as what rank?
Where were you on VE and/or VJ day?

Were there any lighter moments in your war experience?
The answers to these four questions helped to inform a decision on whether the person should be asked for an interview when compared with information on other possible contributors.

In principle, would you be willing to do an interview with us about your experiences in the war?
Do you live near enough London to travel there and back in a day or will you be staying overnight and if so, where?
This determines when the person could be interviewed and may raise the possibility of interviewing them at their hotel.

Do you know anyone else who is coming to the commemorations?
Do you know anyone else who did...
(If they are unwilling or unable to be interviewed.)

Antoinette Graves, freelance researcher

People agree to appear in programmes primarily for one of the following reasons:

- publicity for themselves or their cause;
- to represent a strongly held point of view on an issue;
- because they have a grievance;
- because they are proud of their achievements;
- because they feel others will learn/benefit from their experience.

Deciding what their motive might be will help if they are reluctant to appear. In general, however, if they are less than totally committed, you need to consider how essential to the programme they are. Could someone else be found to represent a viewpoint, illustrate a situation or tell the kind of story you need?

While working on a consumer programme, I found a woman who had nearly died of carbon monoxide poisoning from a faulty gas fire. I tried to persuade her to appear by saying that her experience might warn others and so prevent further accidents but she was still reluctant.

> I asked whether any relations or friends who were involved in the story might be willing to be interviewed: we needed the human interest/emotional story as well as the official version. In fact, she then agreed to do the interview herself.
>
> *Antoinette Graves, freelance researcher*

Those who want to put their point across may be very difficult if they sense that you are also going to present alternative views and may refuse to appear if their personal or professional enemy is also going to be interviewed. Some, however, will be very happy to represent the awkward squad.

> One of my most rewarding experiences was persuading Dr J. Enoch Powell to take part in a three-way discussion about Judas Iscariot for a programme going out at Easter. For controversy, I wanted someone who believed that Judas was not a traitor but a good and decent man.
>
> There were several routes to try, including:
>
> 1. Had anyone written a book about this?
> 2. Theological departments at universities;
> 3. Hebrew translators.
>
> At lunch-time, I walked round some bookshops to see what books had been written on the subject. Not finding anything useful, I browsed around for my own interests and came across Enoch Powell's autobiography. I'd always associated him with racism because of his 'Rivers of Blood' speech and, as an Asian who'd arrived in this country a few years after it, I was curious to know more about his views. There was a summary of his life which included that he'd learned Urdu and was, in fact, passionate about India.
>
> Back in the office, I looked him up in *Who's Who*, where I gathered he was heavily involved in theological research. What had started out as a personal interest was rapidly turning into a piece of serendipity. I got his telephone number, but was nervous of calling him because I was worried that someone so knowledgeable

on the subject and known for his intellectual ferocity, might expect me to answer in-depth questions relating to the subject – if I couldn't it would reflect badly on both me and the BBC.

When I finally plucked up enough courage, I dialled the number. His very characteristic voice answered, 'Who is it that wishes to speak to Mr Powell?' I gave the BBC and my name, but worried that my Asian name might cause problems. He said, 'It is I speaking'. (As if I hadn't recognised his voice!)

He asked me about my name, and my origins and chatted happily and humorously for a while about his time in India. I then asked him his views on Judas. They were exactly what I needed – Judas was not a traitor, without him Jesus would not have been crucified; therefore Judas sacrificed his reputation and was altruistic in his actions and to this day wrongly accused of being a traitor. Mr Powell agreed to appear on the programme (in his words, the BBC fee was worth thirty pieces of silver).

The whole experience of contacting him and discussing the subject got me over the hurdle of thinking that any experts I phone will expect me to have as much knowledge about the subject as they do. It was the first time I'd spoken directly to anyone whom I regarded as a historical figure with a penetratingly deep intellect and I came away realising they are not out to intimidate researchers or give us a hard time, but are often happy to provide us with as much information as possible. Surprisingly, many of the guests are very humble and flattered we should think them experts.

Ashe Hussain, freelance radio producer

The research interview

If, based on the initial conversations, you decide you need to meet people to do a more in-depth interview, arrange a time, date and place. Give some indication of how long you expect the interview to take. It may be advisable to confirm the arrangements by letter. Ensure that you know how to get there. If they are not used to dealing with the media, write to confirm

why you are meeting and the arrangements. This makes it easier for them to understand what you want and should also reassure them about your professional credentials.

In television, it is usual to meet contributors before they are filmed, except if they are already experienced in appearing on screen or in current affairs programmes with a very short time-scale where there may only be a telephone call to decide how well they will come across either in a recording or a studio appearance. With inexperienced interviewees, the aim of the research interview is partly to find out what kind of contribution they will make and partly to see them. In an ideal world, it should not matter what people look like but viewers will be distracted from what is being said if the interviewee has an unusual appearance or some physical mannerism, like a facial tic. It is also an opportunity to gauge how the interviewee is likely to react to being recorded. There is, however, no foolproof method of knowing who will be intimidated by recording and who will sail through it, no matter how confident they appear at the research interview.

In radio what you hear is what you get so the decision to record a contributor will be made on the telephone call alone. As tape is much cheaper than a full film crew, radio interviews are usually recorded at the first meeting. There are advantages to both methods. A filmed interview will give the potential contributor time to think over what to say but the freshness and immediacy of recording first thoughts may be lost.

Real people programmes are often more difficult. They're not people who've got their spiel and are used to giving what's expected but have got to be quite natural talking about themselves. Radio is easier than television, you know what you've got from the telephone conversation, but you can't always predict their reactions on air. I was the producer on *Ad Lib*, a programme on Radio 4 in which people from a particular profession – plastic surgeons, publicans, whatever – discussed their work and what they thought about it with Robert Robinson. My job was to select people and then write briefing notes, a profile of each for RR. If you've got enough people, the others will compensate if one is overcome and doesn't talk.

Geoff Prout, freelance assistant producer

Preparing for the interview

The research meeting has two purposes: the first is effectively to audition potential contributors for a television programme or video production but the second is to gain their confidence. Dress, posture and manner will all contribute to the impression created. Research has shown that most people form their views on those they meet within the first fifteen seconds. Although the interviewee will have some impression of you and your company from the initial telephone call, this will be added to when you meet. What impression do you want to give?

Although you will already have done some research into the subject, you may need to do more and to consider carefully what you want from the meeting and to structure it. Think of an interview as a conversation, but a conversation with a point. In social situations you might find yourself meeting someone about whom you have already heard a great deal. You do not, in general, plunge into the most interesting and scandalous aspect immediately. 'So what's this I hear about you and sheep?' is guaranteed to stop any conversation dead in its tracks if it's the first question. It's the same for research interviews. Lead up to the important questions gradually.

Conversations, job interviews, research interviews for television – even some police interviews of suspects – all follow a similar structure. There is usually a little of what is called in linguistics phatic communion: 'Hello', 'Nice weather', 'Did you have a good journey?' or similar. These do not convey information but are designed to signal good will and to gain the trust of the person. You don't, obviously, have to script these in advance but you do need to think about the kind of questions you will ask and the order in which you ask them.

Factual answers are easy for the interviewee to answer, so the interview proper starts off with them. This is not a waste of time but will help to confirm, refute or add to research already done. Consider which parts of the research you have already done need more detail. When the interviewee has gained confidence and trust, you can go on to areas that are more speculative or which involve beliefs, emotions and opinions. You may also need to prepare in advance the exact phrasing of particular questions, especially those which are on sensitive areas.

Any sentence starting How…? Who…? What…? Why…? When…? and Where…? will lead to an open reply, giving more than a one-word answer. This is particularly useful

for the preliminary research interview because it gives you more material to select from when you come to record the interview on camera. If you ask a closed question such as 'Has any research been done on this medical problem?', you may get a simple 'No', which closes the subject. But if you ask 'What kind of research has been done in this area?', you may get a reply along the lines of 'Research has been done on other auto-immune diseases which have implications for this one but nothing on this particular illness'. This will open up at least two new lines of questioning you might otherwise have missed, i.e. what implications and why no research on this disease.

Consider also how different phrasing will affect the answer:

'What do you think will happen…?'
'What do you feel will happen…?'
'How do you see the situation developing…?'

The reply to each of these will be subtly different. The first invites a reasoned analysis, the second a gut reaction and the third a speculative forecast. Once you've started each area of interest with an open question, you can then follow up by asking questions requiring a more precise answer, perhaps by offering alternatives: 'Does this mean…or…?' or something that does require a simple 'yes' or 'no'; but these should not be prepared in advance – when the interview takes place you will be listening and thinking about the implications.

The method of recording the interview must be decided. Tape recorders are the favoured method of many researchers: they give an accurate record of what was said and this might be essential if the subject is very complex or controversial. Sometimes, however, a recorder can put a barrier between interviewer and interviewee, especially if it's an interview with someone not accustomed to talking to the media. A simple notebook might be more appropriate but sitting scribbling does have unfortunate connotations of 'Everything you say may be taken down…' and will also put a barrier between you and the person you're talking to. You will also break eye contact when you look down to write.

If you are using a tape recorder, check that it works, that you have spare batteries and that you know how to operate the equipment. If you are worried about the machine, you cannot concentrate on the interview nor will it help to create the right impression. If you are making written notes, does your pen work,

have you got enough pencils? Do you need to take anything else with you for the interview, photographs for examples or copies of anything that you might want to quote from? If you're also considering locations, should you take a camera? If you take everything you might want for every eventuality, are you going to look like the last refugee out of a war zone?

Appearances are important. You need to look professional but not intimidating. The idea should be to show the interviewee that they have been considered and for some people casual clothes will be appropriate. Not too casual, however, and never anything that is less than spotlessly clean. When in doubt, dress up slightly to show an effort has been made. Where is the meeting to be? Is your footwear suitable if you're going to be outside on a building site or in a garden, for example?

Manner must also be appropriate. For meeting a busy tycoon, brisk professionalism might be the keynote to show recognition that time is valuable. A gentler, less dynamic approach is needed to talk to someone unused to interviews or when considering a sensitive subject.

Conducting the interview

Whatever the kind of interviewee, however, a few minutes small talk is essential to ease both parties into the interview proper. Follow the structure you have already prepared but don't work rigidly down your list of questions or areas for discussion. Pursue interesting sidelines without losing sight of all the points to be covered. Try, however, not to make it too obvious that there is a list. Remember, this is a conversation and the relationship you should be building up with the interviewee will be jeopardised if you keep consulting a piece of paper. If a tape recorder is being used, put it to one side, not between you and the interviewee and then, as far as possible, forget about it.

Although the aim is to hold a conversation, the interviewee is the most important factor. Your views and experiences are, generally, not of interest and you may alienate or irritate the person you're talking to if you express them. There are exceptions to this. If you are working on a sensitive subject, interviewees may be more forthcoming if they know you share or can understand their experiences.

Do not argue with interviewees, however misguided, repulsive or just plain wrong what they say is. You might need to

suggest that there are opposing views to elicit responses but this must be phrased neutrally. 'They say...' is often a lazy journalist's way of putting personal opinions and lays you open to the response, 'Who says...?'. Consider carefully which sources of information or views you choose to quote. On the other hand, be careful about expressing agreement. If both sides of an argument are to be included in the final programme, contributors may feel betrayed if they were led to believe only their views would be represented.

Body language and posture are also important when you meet the interviewee. Hunching yourself defensively with crossed arms does not promote an atmosphere of trust. Sprawling backwards with your arms and legs spread out does not, however, suggest ease but superiority. If you are carrying a bulging briefcase or a lot of paraphernalia, try to leave it outside the room where you are doing the interview, along with your overcoat, scarves, hats and other extraneous clothing. These might suggest that you are too rushed to give the interviewee your full attention and they will make you look like a stranger.

There's a technique known as active listening which helps both establish a good relationship with interviewees and ensure that you are getting what they say right. Feedback to the interviewees what you understand them to have said in slightly different words. This needs care to avoid putting words in their mouth or directing the interview in a direction that might not be a fair representation of the interviewee's position, especially in controversial or sensitive areas. Someone who feels they have been badly treated can be further inflamed if you up the ante by what you say, for example: 'You must have been really angry...how awful...and then, I suppose, you felt really betrayed...'. This is very unethical.

Given the luxury of a captive audience, someone who appears totally fascinated by them, many interviewees will ramble or take the opportunity to say everything they have wanted to say for a long time. You need to balance the need to get a full picture against wasting time on irrelevancies. When doing a research interview for later recording, there's a case for letting them get it all off their chests now rather than later. A researcher's time is cheaper than a full crew's.

An interview for radio is different because the final version is being recorded. You can suggest the need for concision by your questions: 'In a few words, why...?' 'Can you sum that

up?'. You can also speed them up by your body language, breaking eye contact, opening your mouth as if you're about to speak (but not actually saying anything which would cause editing problems), shifting in your chair and so on. An increasing number of people in official positions, however, are going on media training courses that teach them to have their say, come hell, high water or all the hints the interviewer is dropping. In extreme cases, you can try peering at the tape recorder with a worried expression to suggest that their words are not being recorded for posterity.

The interview will probably come to a natural conclusion. Do not leap up, switch off the tape recorder and leave immediately you have got a good, emotional story or a controversial opinion. You don't want to leave potential contributors in a highly wrought state, wondering if they have said too much or the wrong thing to someone who is, after all, a stranger from the media. They must feel secure and, of course, trust you. So go back to factual matters.

Check you can come back if you need any further information or details and, if this is for later recording, on availability without committing yourself to a definite agreement that the interviewee will appear. This might be the right time to ask people to reconsider any requests made for anonymity or for certain things to be off-the-record. You will have gained an impression about how best to phrase this kind of request and they, in turn, should have made up their minds about your trustworthiness.

The interview, however, does not stop until you have left the building. People are often more forthcoming and will say something important when they believe the interview is over, so leave the tape running while you wind up the session and note immediately anything else of interest said while you are being escorted to the lift or the door. If you are interviewing someone at their place of work, remember that secretaries, receptionists and doormen may well report back anything you said to or asked them.

Writing up the interview

However you have chosen to record the interview, on tape or by making notes, you will need to add to this as soon as possible after the interview has finished. How does the person come across, were there any points at which body language told you something that what was said didn't? If you're interviewing several people in a day, make notes on each instantly: you

may think you'll remember but immediate impressions will be blurred by subsequent conversations.

The whole interview or part of the interview may need to be transcribed. Alternatively, a summary of what was said, noting any particular points of interest, may be enough. Add your impressions of and suggestions about how the interviewee could be used which you can discuss later with the rest of the team. Highlight any good anecdotes or opinions that can be elicited at the recording.

Issuing contracts to contributors

When it has been decided which contributors are to be used in the programme, the circumstances associated with their appearance will have to be agreed. Sometimes this is just done on the telephone or by a simple, standard form, letter or fax. Alternatively, a special contract may need to be drawn up, especially if an actor or a musician to whom special union rates may apply is being used. If there are special arrangements to be made, it is best to put them in writing.

Matters for consideration and confirmation, either verbally or in writing, will include the following:

- Fee (if any) and expenses.
- Dates and details of the appearance or recording, the time and place.
- Transport: will this be provided or will the interviewees make their own arrangements? You may need to organise parking space if they are coming in their own cars.
- Accommodation: if the interviewee needs to stay overnight, you may have to organise a room somewhere.
- Consent: does your contributor need anyone's permission to appear? Special arrangements apply to children, especially if they are to give a performance.
- Health and safety: are there any special facilities that have to be organised, e.g. wheelchair access, protective clothing etc.
- Programme credits: as well as checking the spelling and details of the name, title or position and organisation, there may be an acknowledgement to be included in the end credits.

4
ACQUIRING AND USING VISUAL AND AUDIO MATERIAL

Although information and people remain the bedrock of all news and documentary programmes, there is a limit to the number of talking heads the viewer or listener will endure. Television, in particular, requires a variety of visual elements

to sustain interest. Sound, though often low on the list of considerations, can considerably enhance a production.

Authenticity, convenience, expense

Archive material is used for three reasons:

- authenticity;
- convenience;
- expense.

Authenticity. The audience may need to see, or hear, rather than have described a situation or an event. Archive footage of, for example, an event in the past will add to understanding of the event – remember the old journalists' dictum 'Every picture is worth a thousand words'. The sound of an air-raid siren recaptures the atmosphere of wartime for older people. The way people talk has changed considerably within the last thirty years: footage of people speaking, either on film or sound alone, is a reminder of what people thought and how they expressed those thoughts in the past.

Even on a documentary programme, a voice-over, either by a narrator or by the subject of the programme recorded on a wild track containing factual information, will be better than just a talking head. Rather than, for example, seeing an elderly woman say she was born in Leeds in the 1930s, the eldest of six children, you should consider getting archive film of Leeds at that time, perhaps with children playing in the street, and lay her voice giving these kind of factual details over it. Alternatively, there might be a still photograph of her family you could use.

Some programmes use footage from television companies around the world, not only to report current events but to demonstrate how funny foreigners are. Others use amateur recordings of domestic disasters. Again, the original must be obtained: simply describing what happened or re-enacting it in the studio would not produce the same effect of authenticity.

Convenience. There may not be the time to go and film events or a place may currently be inaccessible for political reasons. This particularly applies to news, which uses a great deal of archive footage called up from a library. Distance may

also be a consideration and sometimes this is a matter of convenience; sometimes it is a question of the third category.

Expense. It may be too expensive to send a film crew or a photographer to a place, but library footage or stills of, for example, South America will show everything from Aztec temples to current living conditions there.

Having decided what additional material is needed to illustrate a story, the next determination to be made is whether to buy, licence or commission. This is all to do with rights rather than the material itself. Buying is self-explanatory: the production pays a fee to whoever owns the material. It can then do whatever it wants with the pictures or sound and can sell or license its use to other organisations. Licensing is, in effect, hiring the material for a specific purpose. The production signs a contract with the organisation or person owning the material to use it under certain conditions, which usually include the number of times it may be shown, in which parts of the world, or territories, it may be shown and what fee will be payable. This will depend on the type of production and size of audience expected. Something intended for broadcasting on one of the mass media channels will attract a higher cost than a video intended for training purposes within a few companies. In general, costs for educational programmes are lower. Commissioning material means employing someone to produce exactly what is needed.

Buying the right to use something is the most straightforward alternative but is not always possible. Libraries make their living from licensing material: they are not lightly going to give up a potential source of income. If, however, you are getting something from a private source, try to buy the right for its use outright. It will make repeats and sales elsewhere much easier.

In 1995 the world's media were at the historic occasion when the USA's President, Bill Clinton, met and shook hands with Gerry Adams, leader of Ireland's Sinn Fein. Unfortunately, they somehow all missed capturing this event. Two amateurs, one with a still camera, the other with his camcorder, did manage to get pictures. The rights to the video footage were bought outright for a very small fee.

If it is going to be too expensive or too restrictive to license a still photograph or sound, it may be cheaper and less time-consuming to commission a photographer or musicians to

produce exactly what's wanted. Ensure that the production retains the copyright on the work produced in the contract that is drawn up. In some situations, it might be preferable, or even necessary, to hire an artist to draw a picture. This is most common when reporting court cases, because cameras of any kind are not currently allowed at trials.

Still pictures

Picture libraries hold colour and black and white photographs, either prints or negatives, from which a print will have to be made and paid for, whether it is included or not in the final production. Many also have transparencies. Check which is the most suitable format to obtain, depending on the way it is to be used.

If only part of the picture is to be featured or a move across it in a simple way is needed, this can be done on location or in the studio with a cameraman/woman at the same time as the rest of the recording. When something more complicated, such as changing the colour or co-ordinating camera movements with music, is needed, specialist rostrum camera facilities will have to be booked and the pictures taken there. In news programmes and for doing some graphics sequences a slide scanner may be used. This is a fixed electronic camera which projects, as the name implies, transparencies. Check whether the picture you need is for use in a slide scanner.

When selecting the pictures to be used, find out where in the production they are to be included. Newspaper photographs are intended to add information to the printed text or even sum up the whole story. News programmes particularly may need something less dramatic, perhaps just a head-and-shoulders, studio portrait of a person as a visual reminder of who is being mentioned. A detailed photograph would distract viewers from what is being said. Alternatively, an informal picture may be needed to illustrate something in the script. 'He and his second wife met at a party given by Scott and Zelda Fitzgerald in Paris' would need to show the couple at a party, ideally with one or both of the Fitzgeralds. In a really ideal world, of course, moving pictures would be best for this situation.

It's always better to go along to a library if at all possible: however well the context is explained to the librarian

or researcher there, he/she will not have the detailed knowledge of where and how a still is going to be included. Libraries have different ways of working: some allow people to take a selection of pictures away with them, others require prints (which will have to be paid for) to be made from negatives.

Keeping track of pictures, especially if your production is using a large number, is essential. A chart must be prepared, listing (as a minimum, although the actual content and layout will vary to include precisely the knowledge you and the production need) the picture, the source, the date it was taken, the copyright owner (who may not be the library, so check this), the fee, where and how the picture is to be used, the spool number of any tape on which it is recorded and other miscellaneous information, like restrictions on use. Cardboard-backed envelopes to keep pictures undamaged are essential.

This is a complex area. This section cannot hope to cover all aspects of a film researcher's job: it's a book in itself. If only short inserts presenting few problems are required, however, this will fall within the remit of general programme research. If the film research required is extensive or might present problems, a specialist should be used. Dealing with overseas archives brings additional complications.

When dealing with overseas film archives, remember time zone differences and also that working hours in other countries may be different from here: many start early in the morning and finish mid-afternoon. You can waste a lot of time if you ring when they're at lunch or after they've closed.

Maurice Raine, freelance film researcher

Apart from the major film libraries, many large companies, such as Sainsbury's, and organisations, like trades unions, have their own archives and there are also individual collectors and amateur film-makers. There is such a vast amount of film kept in archives all over the world that looking for a particular reel can seem like a needle-in-a-haystack job.

In film research, too, a chart should be prepared to keep track of the material being used: the date of the footage, duration of clip, the content in the form of a shot list, the source, the copyright owner, the format, details of transfer (including the spool number), cost and miscellaneous information, like restrictions on use, need to be included as a minimum.

> Always keep your paperwork immaculate and keep a record of all your dealings on a particular job – that way there are fewer nasty surprises and you are often the only person on the production team who is keeping their head while all about you are running around like headless chickens.
>
> *Jane Mercer, film researcher*
>
> (This applies to all research!)

Documentary footage is relatively easy to obtain and pay for. Feature films are more complicated and may need extra time to arrange, especially if the clip you want to use is from a non-current production. The reasons for this are given in the section on copyright.

Time spent browsing through information about film and videotape archives and getting to know the staff is not wasted. The more knowledge a researcher holds in his or her head, the less time will be wasted looking for it in printed sources, or making a series of fruitless telephone calls, often against the clock.

> When President John Kennedy was assassinated in 1963 I heard the first report about it on radio and immediately rang the Presentation Department at Rediffusion, one of the then ITV companies. I rushed down to the Rediffusion library and pulled out everything suitable for a full-scale, in mourning transmission for the rest of the night. I also knew someone who was dubbing a documentary about Kennedy and I went to his cutting room for that. Rediffusion took all their programmes off the air to do an extended programme on Kennedy while the BBC went on transmitting things like *The Harry Worth Show* (this was

> a popular, rather whimsical, comedy).
>
> A few years later, in 1968, I was rung by Jeremy Isaacs at six-thirty in the morning. 'King's been assassinated,' he said. My first thought, at that time of day, was to wonder why someone would want to kill Cecil King, who'd resigned from the Daily Mirror the night before. Once I'd sorted out that it was Martin Luther King who was dead, I went straight down to the American Embassy because I knew, as many people don't, that they have a lot of material on site, to take everything before the BBC or anyone else could get there. I pulled out everything, including the famous 'I have a dream...' speech. On both occasions, it helped that I was friendly with both the American cultural attaché and the librarian at the Embassy.
>
> *Maurice Raine, freelance film researcher*

There are large, general archives, both national and regional, as well as commercial libraries. Some specialise in what's called stock footage: clips of generic subjects like aeroplanes, animals or countries. These are useful when specially shot footage is either too expensive or too inconvenient to obtain.

Others are the archives of newsreel companies: organisations that used to make the short packages that formed a standard part of cinema programmes until the 1970s. Before the advent of television, the cinema was where people went to see the news both in this country and abroad.

> For *Women at War*, the production team had filmed a woman who, as a girl, had seen Hitler at one of his rallies during the early 1920s, long before he became the German leader. I asked the German Bundesarchiv (the national film archive) for all the early Hitler rallies and found film of the actual rally which matched the interview she'd already done.
>
> *Maurice Raine, freelance film researcher*

This was not an event that seemed important enough to have been covered by British newsreel companies but in Germany was newsworthy.

There are also specialist archives: the Imperial War Museum is the most obvious example but there are others, often very

small and contained within a larger organisation, like a museum, which will also hold still photographs and objects.

Wallpaper

News bulletins on television may need general rather than specific footage. This is known as wallpaper – moving pictures over which the news item is read. It's not quite a question of 'never mind the quality, measure the length' but often it is a matter of getting whatever is already available in the company's library or can be quickly obtained featuring the subject of the news item.

When Camilla Parker-Bowles, the Prince of Wales' mistress, and her husband announced their divorce, it was impossible to get specially shot footage of any of the major figures in the story. The archives were trawled and came up with footage previously shot of Mrs Parker-Bowles at a hunt (in fact, only about six minutes of her had ever been recorded at that time), her husband at an auction, and the Prince of Wales in recent documentaries about him and on the ski slopes from a news item made a few days previously. These were assembled and the background to the story read over the footage. This was supplemented with still photographs and graphics. The only footage shot on the day was of the reporter who produced the story and a general view of the deserted Parker-Bowles' house. The end result was visually rather incoherent but both the BBC and ITN did professional jobs with remarkably little material.

Licensing footage

When the programme is completed, details of all the footage (including duration) from a library that was used in the pro-gramme are recorded and sent back to the library which then issues an invoice. An agreement recording the terms and conditions is made. Ensure that clearance of all material in the clip, e.g. music, quotations from published work, etc. is made and any residual fees due to performers are covered. The library should have details of these but you still need to check them.

Formats

When obtaining footage, always ask in which formats the library holds the material. There may be a choice so you can obtain a

Table 4.1 Film formats

Date	Size[1]	Notes
1895	51 mm	Widescreen format
1898+	17.5 mm	
1900	75 mm	Lumiere
1904		*Sprockets began to be punched by manufacturer, rather than customer*
1909	35 mm	Edison format adopted as standard
1914	70 mm	Panoramica, later reduced to horizontal 35 mm
1923	9.5 mm	
1923	16 mm	
1927	35 mm	Cinemascope, used anamorphic lenses requiring special projection and transfer facilities[2]
1927	35 mm	Polyvision, 2 x 35 mm frames projected simultaneously
1912	28 mm	Reduced from 35 mm
1932	8 mm	Amateur format
1937		*Television began in Britain. It could use film shot with a conventional camera, passed immediately through the developing process, then scanned and transmitted in under a minute. Few recordings of early, live transmissions survive*
1951	35 mm	Safety stock for professional use introduced and universally adopted almost immediately
1958		*Telerecording, a method of recording the output of an electronic studio on to film, was introduced. Some programmes survive only in this form*
1960	3 mm	USAF, used in space
1966	Super 8	Mainly an amateur format
1968		*Colour television began*
1990	Super 16	Uses 40% more image area than standard 16 mm

[1]   In the early days, there were experiments with a number of different sizes, which continued even after the Edison format had been adopted as standard.

[2]   Other formats use anamorphic lenses: this was the first.

copy that can be incorporated into your production with a minimum of complicated or expensive transfer time. Film is, in many ways, easier to transfer than videotape, especially if the videotape comes in an obsolete form. As the technicians say, film is future-proof, which means there will always be a way of shining a light through a translucent medium to re-record the images. Electronic media, however, usually need the original equipment for which the format was made to reproduce the sound and pictures. It should be established early on which facilities will have to be specially booked. The main formats a non-specialist researcher is likely to encounter are outlined below.

Film is available in 35 mm, 16 mm, Super 16 and Super 8 formats. There were, in addition, a bewildering variety of sizes in the early days (see Table 4.1), but most of the experimentation was used for feature films. Copies for cinemas or amateur film societies without the necessary equipment to show, for example, 3-D films may also have been made.

Film can come with the sound on a separate magnetic track (sep-mag) or with the sound on a strip running alongside the pictures (com-opt). The former is easier to use if it needs to be heavily edited or a new commentary is going to be put on something which already contains music or sound effects. Ask if there is a separate M&E (music and effects) track. If the sound has been mixed down to leave only one track with words, music and effects all together (as it is in com-opt prints) it is virtually impossible to isolate the different elements and delete one of them.

Before 1951, professional 35 mm film was recorded on nitrate stock, which is highly flammable and special arrangements have to be made for its transfer. After that date, safety stock was used by professionals. It had been used for amateur footage (16 mm or 8 mm) from the earliest times, but its tendency to warp made it unsuitable for professional use. Most commercial libraries have now transferred their nitrate stock footage to less flammable material but you may still find some, either in libraries or in private hands, and you should be aware of the problems.

The aspect ratio between the width and height of a frame is different in the cinema from that used in television. In cinema it is 5:4; in television 4:3. This creates problems in showing feature films on television. A black band appears at the top

Table 4.2 Video formats[1]

Year	Format	Signal	On	Size	Notes
1956	2 inch	Analogue	Open reel	2 inch	Also known as Quad. Cannot be viewed when spooling forward or back
1969	U-matic hi-band	Analogue	Cassette	3/4 inch	Used for ENG (electronic news gathering)
1969	U-matic lo-band	Analogue	Cassette	3/4 inch	Used for off-line editing
1969	U-matic hi-band SP	Analogue	Cassette	3/4 inch	
1971	1 inch B format	Analogue	Open reel	1 inch	
1972	2 inch C format	Analogue	Open reel	1 inch	
1976	VHS	Analogue	Cassette	1/2 inch	Domestic format
1985	Betacam	Analogue	Cassette	1/2 inch	Used for PSC (portable single camera) recording on location
1987	D1	Digital	Cassette	3/4 inch	Broadcast format
1988	D2	Digital	Cassette	3/4 inch	Broadcast format
1988	S-VHS	Analogue	Cassette	1/2 inch	Domestic format
1989	HI-8	Analogue	Cassette	1/2 inch	Domestic format
1989	Betacam SP	Analogue	Cassette	1/2 inch	
1990	D3	Digital	Cassette	1/2 inch	Broadcast format
1992	DCT	Digital	Cassette	3/4 inch	Mainly used for post-production
1993	HDVS/HDD 1000	Digital	Open reel	1 inch	
1993	D5	Digital	Cassette	1/2 inch	Broadcast format
1994	Digital Betacam	Digital	Cassette	1/2 inch	
1996	DVC	Digital	Cassette	1/4 inch	
1996	DVC Pro	Digital	Cassette	1/4 inch	
1996	Mini-DVC	Digital	Cassette	1/4 inch	
1996	Digital S	Digital	Cassette	1/2 inch	
1996	Sony DV	Digital	Cassette	1/4 inch	Domestic format, also used by professionals
1996	DVCAM	Digital	Cassette	1/4 inch	
1997	Betacam SX	Digital	Cassette	1/4 inch	

These are the main formats that a researcher will encounter but, especially in the early days of video there were others which had either a limited or specialised function, e.g. closed circuit video.

Table 4.3 TV standards

Name of system	Major countries using it	No. of frames per second	No. of lines
PAL[1] (Phase Alternating Line)	Great Britain, most of Europe, Australia	25	625
NTSC (National Television Systems Committee)	USA, Japan	24	525
SECAM (Sequence Couleur A Memoire)	France, Russia, Eastern Europe	25	625

[1] PAL M (used in parts of South America) and PALplus are developments of this system.

and bottom of the screen: this is called letterboxing. It can be corrected on transfer but there is some loss of the picture.

As well as the aspect ratio there are other technical problems when transferring feature film clips for incorporation into a programme. Some film formats use anamorphic lenses to squeeze a wider image on to the standard 35 mm film and require special projection equipment to show the film.

Videotape

Early videotape imitated film in that it came on an open reel. When transferring these, extra time must be allowed to set them up. Videotape now comes on cassettes in a number of formats both for professional and domestic use. Companies tend to acquire equipment that is state-of-the-art when the time comes to refit their studios or edit suites but they do not necessarily change everything when a new system comes along. Table 4.2 shows the date when the commoner formats first became available, but remember that some organisations may still be using a format invented fifteen or more years ago.

In addition to those examples shown, there were many others which appeared briefly or were confined to one particular market. In the early 1970s there were three 1 inch helical scan formats produced by competing manufacturers (Shabaden, Sony and Phillips) which were used mainly for

closed-circuit television in educational establishments. So if you're working on a programme about someone who was a teacher and might have been recorded, bear this in mind.

There is a further subdivision: analogue or digital. Reproduction of the former deteriorates with each generation of copies made. The latter does not degrade because it is based on numbers, which remain the same for each generation, rather than copying a signal. This may be an important consideration if extensive editing on linear equipment is required.

If material from overseas is being used, the different television standards used in other parts of the world must be taken into account. Currently there are three, as shown in Table 4.3. These involve different line standards, which is also a consideration when using old videotape recorded in this country. Currently it is 625 lines but before 1964 it was 405 lines, although the frame rate (in this country) of 25 per second was the same as that currently used. Copies of this early material come mostly from transfers to film and are of poor quality but some videotape with better picture quality survives. It was also black and white.

All these problems, both for film and video, mean that anyone doing research must ask which format the original material is on and then either know or find out which facilities are needed to transfer it.

Graphics and animation

It's hard to comprehend statistics and other figures solely through what is said. It is usually, therefore, best done on screen graphically. Animation – making it move – adds interest and can enhance the message. A programme strand will have a house style but if a one-off production is going to contain a number of graphic sequences they should be presented in a consistent way.

This is, however, a technique largely associated with news and studio-based programmes, so a documentary made on location may have to come up with another method: a pie chart dropped suddenly into a sequence shot in someone's office looks incongruous.

A mix from actuality to an animated sequence can be effective, as long as the two match visually. One edition of *Timewatch* showed a reconstruction of how the ancient

temple at Karnak in Egypt probably looked by mixing from the present day ruins to a model. The colour of the model was the same as the stone of the temple and the transition from one to the other, a dissolve, was made on a doorway so both colour and shape corresponded.

Graphics are not confined to figures, they can be used for a variety of purposes, like credit sequences or special effects, and are produced in two ways:

- Computer generated. This is the usual method. There are a variety of machines and the limits to what can be produced are mainly those of time and money.
- Drawn. Although rarer, this is still a technique that can be considered.

Another option is for models to be constructed. But, however the graphics are produced, time needs to be allowed to do them. A simple idea can be a lot more complicated to carry out than it may first appear.

When considering what information needs to be included, remember that a television screen is very small and the monitors in people's homes will not be of such high quality as those used professionally. Keep it simple and with as little detail as possible. Graphics designers prefer a written brief, even if they have discussed in detail what's needed. All information must be checked for accuracy and spelling before handing it over: don't assume the designer will correct any errors. Check it after as well: everyone makes mistakes when working under pressure.

Lateral thinking is often needed when researching graphic material.

> While working on the programme *Women at War*, we needed a map of pre-War Germany for the graphics guy to use. I found that the pre-War map plates had been destroyed, ironically during the Blitz, but rang John Bartholemew himself in Edinburgh and found, as I had hoped, that he still had a file copy.
>
> *Maurice Raine, freelance film researcher*

In this case, time might have been lost in finding out the names of dealers and collectors and then ringing through what would undoubtedly be a long list. The map publishers Bartholemew have been around for many years, so it was a

sensible supposition that the company might have some pre-War material.

Props and models

Like using graphics, the message may be put across better by showing, rather than describing, an object or a process. The simplest props can be obtained by either buying or hiring. If something more complex is needed, such as a representation of the DNA double helix or something to show the inner workings of a machine, a model can be built. The major consideration here is whether the prop or model needs to be what is called 'practical', i.e. it works, or whether it is to be used as a dressing prop. If, for example, the production needs a kitchen on set, do the stove and the sink need to work or are they simply to be in the background? Again, time and money have to be considered. If something is being hired from a commercial supplier, it must be specified whether the object is to be practical or not.

If someone will be demonstrating how an object works, there should always be at least one spare: Murphy's law states that if something can go wrong it will and this applies particularly to props. Presenters and reporters may need to rehearse more than once for a complicated or elaborate process. Continuity is another factor: candles burn down, liquid may be used up, so there must be enough available to ensure that shots will match when cut together.

The safety and insurance aspects of props and models must be taken into account. Fire, smoke, firearms, water, electricity, gas, real money, a very valuable object (like jewellery or a painting), animals and a number of other props will need special arrangements made and the cost of these, as well as that of the prop or model, must be allowed for. A fireman, a handler or a security guard may need to be in attendance and their fees must be included in the calculations. Enquire whether insurance is included in the hire fee or whether it must be arranged separately. The production's own insurance may cover some props but not others.

Records of props used must also be kept: where they came from, what special arrangements for their use need to be made etc. in the same way as for stills and moving pictures.

Some objects are so precious that their owners will not allow them off-site. Access to a museum or historic house may have

to be arranged. If this is going to be a complicated or expensive procedure, check whether a still or moving film of the object already exists and whether obtaining that would be an easier or cheaper option.

Sound

There are two major sources of sound material not available in the shops: the BBC and the British Library National Sound Archive, which also keeps a data base of other sound collections around the country.

There are three kinds of recorded sound:

- Music. The problems here are not so much technical as financial and are largely to do with copyright. Although it can be expensive, this is an area where commissioning a composer of a group of musicians to achieve what you want is worth considering. The British Library National Sound Archive, as well as collecting pre-recorded music, actively records musical performances, particularly jazz to which a whole section there is devoted. It does not, however, hold the rights to the performance, which will still have to be cleared.

- The spoken word. In addition to material available from sound archives, a number of local history projects have an oral history group recording the memories of people in their area. These, however, are usually on domestic quality audio cassettes so may not be of a high enough standard to use for broadcasting. The project organisers may, however, be able to put you in touch with people from the project whom you can re-interview. The British Library National Sound Archive has an extensive collection of recordings from stage productions.

- Sound effects. These are readily available on records and CDs. They are copyrighted but, like mood music, present relatively few clearance problems. If the effect you want is unusual or highly specialised, commissioning should also be considered. The authentic sound of something may not be very impressive and may have to be recreated by the most unlikely means. Rain on a roof, for example, is traditionally produced by using gravel in a tray and horses hooves by coconut shells. The sound may not even exist: the post-nuclear holocaust

sound familiar to audiences is usually represented by a recording of a polar wind. Footsteps may need to be dubbed on to your production because the sync sound did not produce the desired effect. Getting a commercial recording to match exactly is unlikely. There are, however, people who specialise in producing footsteps to match movement, called Foley editors, listed in directories of facilities.

Sound formats

Transferring sound from one format to another is less complicated than dealing with archive footage but again you must check when contacting the source what form the sound recording exists in. There is equipment to improve the quality of very early or damaged records but, as this does not exist in every recording studio, special arrangements must be made. Possible formats you might encounter include:

- vinyl or shellac discs – 78 rpm, 45 rpm, 33.3 rpm;
- compact discs;
- laser discs;
- reel-to-reel magnetic tape;
- cassette audio tapes – analogue or DAT;
- cartridges (known as 'carts') – these are largely used in radio to play jingles and advertisements.

There are other, obsolete methods of sound recording: before tape was invented, a system of recording using wire was around. If material is found in this format, it must be transferred to something that can be incorporated into the production. The British Library National Sound Archive can give advice and can arrange transfer of very old or damaged recordings.

Editing each type of recording presents different problems, depending on the format in which it exists, and this must be built into calculations when booking time. Again, check which alternatives the source holds.

5
ASSESSING AND RECOMMENDING LOCATIONS AND STUDIOS

Although this is a short chapter, the factors to be considered and the questions to be asked are many. Each production will find itself facing different problems: no two recordings are ever quite the same but the ability to anticipate and, if possible

to forestall, problems is the researcher's most useful skill here. Where the recording presents problems, due to time or complexity, expert help should be brought in. There are companies, listed in directories of facilities, that specialise in finding locations and it might be more time- and cost-effective to use one, especially when the needs are very specific or unusual. For productions that present no complications, however, researchers will be expected to assess locations.

While collecting information and considering contributors, you should also be thinking about where recording is to take place. Sometimes this will be dictated by the story or the programme's format, if it is studio-based or done as an outside broadcast.

On location, there is usually an element of choice: a programme about education could be recorded in a number of schools or colleges. The usual practice is to film experts or authority figures in their office so the automatic assumption is that the headteacher will be filmed there. The story might, however, be given more impact by placing the headteacher in a classroom, a playing field or the lavatories (inside or outside). Even if this is not your decision, you can suggest alternatives, and the reasons for them, to the person responsible.

The award-winning documentary *Four Hours in My Lai*, made by Kevin Sim and Michael Bilton for Yorkshire Television, interviewed many of the surviving people, both Vietnamese and American, who were involved in the massacre of the inhabitants of a small village during the Vietnamese war. One of the soldiers who refused to obey orders and kill the villagers, Harry Stanley, was interviewed about why he disobeyed while standing outside in what looks like a timber yard. He appears to be wearing his work clothes. Although this is never explicitly stated, he is plainly a low-paid labourer. The viewer understands, in addition to what he says, that his principled moral stance has, in worldly terms, done him no good at all. However, he has a job: other ex-soldiers interviewed were so traumatised by their experiences that they could not work. Had he been interviewed in his home, like many of the other contributors, the viewer would not draw these inferences.

The major practical considerations connected with locations are:

- Whether the recording is internal, inside either television/film studios or buildings, like a house or office, or external, in the open air.
- Permissions – who owns the site?
- Facilities – what exists on-site and what will need to be brought in?
- Contracts – what are the conditions for its use?

For complicated productions or where recording is likely to take place over a long period, more information about the location or studio than can be obtained by a simple telephone call or visit is needed. Information can come from:

- People – those on site, those who have used the location before.
- Documents – maps, plans, photographs, general information prepared for previous productions.

These are not, however, a substitute for seeing the location. Ideally the director and cameraman/woman should recce the site, not only to look out for the shots that will be needed but also to assess the facilities. If they can't go, it may be the researcher's job to visit the location and report back. It's always a good idea to take a second person, perhaps the production assistant or, in certain circumstances, a safety officer as a second pair of eyes. The latter is especially important if the filming is to take place on water, in the air, at great heights or will involve stunts.

Notes made about the location should be supplemented with photographs (a polaroid camera should be enough) or even a camcorder. These are useful to allow the director to see potential shots, but notes about the facilities – those things which may not be seen on the end product but are vital to the welfare and safety of crew and contributors – need to be added. You also need to think about where the sun and the shade will be at particular times of day. For example, when will the sun be shining through a particular stained glass window in a church? When will the best effects be achieved? When will a spot be in such deep shade that filming is practically impossible?

Facilities

Considerations about facilities apply to studios as well. Here the size of the floor space in relation to the set/s, the number of cameras needed, the lighting rig, the type of equipment in the gallery, machines for playing in VT inserts and recording, whether an audience has to be accommodated etc. must be considered.

The following list applies principally to locations but some will also need to be considered when studios are chosen.

- Transport and parking. If you will be using rail or ferry services, check timetables carefully: they tend to alter according to the time of year. Although crews usually make their own way to the location, where parking is difficult it may be better to hire a transit van for everyone. If using a studio, how will the contributors and perhaps audience be brought there?

- Accommodation and catering. If the production team or any of the contributors has to stay overnight, where will they sleep? Can meals be bought near the location or will some form of on-site catering need to be provided?

- Facilities, e.g. medical, vets, public telephones, garages, toilets. Will anyone involved need special facilities, e.g. a toilet that can accommodate a wheelchair?

- Power supply. Is there electricity on site, how is it produced, will a generator be needed?

- Special equipment. Standard equipment cannot be used in certain environments, e.g. in mines or anywhere there is the danger of an explosion, or in operating theatres where a sterile atmosphere must be maintained.

- Safety equipment, e.g. harnesses for working at heights, hard hats, ear defenders etc. may also be necessary.

- Additional equipment, like lenses, camera mountings, tracks for moving shots (and, if you need these, what is the ground at the outside location like?).

- Weather. What is it likely to be and what alternatives are there if the conditions are too bad for outside recording?

- Local events like a demonstration or a festival (unless that's what is being filmed). Not only will the noise cause problems with recording, but transport and parking will also be difficult.
- Airfields and other noisy industrial and commercial operations.
- Factories, schools and local businesses that might be affected by or disturb filming and whose co-operation you will need.
- Any unusual acoustic effect, e.g. echoes.

Recording on location is a disruptive process. The police need to be informed of any filming and what is involved. If the production is reconstructing something like a robbery, a whole set of complications arise. It doesn't matter how obvious the film crew is, there will always be a good citizen who alerts the police to what appears to be a crime and there are things that cannot be done in a public place, especially where guns or replica guns are involved.

Streets might need to be closed off for a period (this is where police co-operation is essential) and people other than those being filmed can be inconvenienced. Make sure that everyone is informed and warned of the ways in which they might be affected without overemphasising the drawbacks. This can vary from putting a note through doors to calling a meeting of local residents if a great deal of co-operation over a long period is required. Try to find out if any roadworks are planned or if the street is going to be dug up at the time of the recording: the local council should be able to supply this kind of information.

Dealing with the public

Filming usually attracts a crowd, often containing small children who want to jump up and down in front of the camera shouting 'Hello, Mum' or who interrupt shots by calling out 'BBC is rubbish', or 'ITV is stupid', depending on where the crew comes from. They are generally puzzled by independent productions. This needs to be remembered while doing a recce. Additional help to deal with the public might be necessary in a very busy area.

Sometimes an appeal to children's better natures and an explanation of what is happening will keep them quiet. In term time, you can also ask why they aren't in school and threaten them with the police if this doesn't work. If you are recording near a school, it's a good idea to schedule outside shots at times when the children won't be arriving or leaving, when they might interrupt the production. Parents delivering or collecting their offspring at the school gates will also create problems with transport and parking.

Children are not the only ones who can be difficult. When you are recording in a public place, like a park, there are always people with someone they ought not to be with. They can be very difficult if they realise their indiscretions may appear on screen in front of millions of people and this is another occasion on which you might consider taking along extra help to deal with the public.

Permissions and licences

Almost everywhere filming takes place will require permission from some person or organisation and this may take time to obtain. You will need to find out who owns the site where you hope to work and how long the process takes. Filming in the street should be notified to the local police. This is usually called getting police permission. Although, in theory, it is not permission that has to be obtained, the production can fall foul of a number of laws, causing a public nuisance, obstruction etc., so it is advisable to gain the police's co-operation before going out with a crew. Radio is easier: one or two people with a tape recorder and hand-held microphone are unlikely to cause any major problems, unless the recording is being made in sensitive circumstances, like a riot or public demonstration.

Trespassing on land is another grey area: theoretically trespassers can only be taken to court if they cause damage. Trespass is a civil matter, not criminal, so it would be the owner of a property who would take any proceedings, although the police can be summoned to help remove intruders.

Minor or major alterations to the location may have to be made. There is usually a clause in any contract where this is necessary to the effect that the place will be restored to its previous condition. Whether the production team is responsible

or a company specialising in this kind of work is hired will have to be arranged.

Filming on water, whether inland or at sea, brings in a whole set of separate problems. Permission is usually still needed and special safety equipment, like life jackets and safety harnesses, even if the crew will be filming from land, should be obtained. The water should also be tested if there is any chance of someone falling in or if someone will intentionally be in the water. There are a whole range of diseases that can be carried in water, as well as pollution hazards.

Tides and currents have to be researched and not only if you will be at sea. You need to check if the stretch of a river you will be working on is tidal. Any boats you hire should have insurance but this may not cover the production team. Check the terms of the boat and its crew's insurance.

Insurance is also a major consideration when filming from the air, another potentially dangerous situation. If any complicated filming is to take place, permission must be obtained from the Civil Aviation Authority. There may be restrictions on the route that can be taken and the height at which you can fly.

Contracts

Even if a fee is not being paid, a contract should still be issued for the use of a location to make sure that the production's insurance will cover any accident or damage that may occur. All productions must have insurance against, among other factors, damage to property or injury to the public.

A contract will also protect the production if the person or organisation has a change of heart about participating. Foot-in-the-door journalism is the exception to this. When the contract is drawn up, try to make sure every eventuality is covered: whose responsibility will security on the site be and whose responsibility is it to restore the site to its original condition if any changes have to be made?

6
THE SCRIPT

The commentary on a documentary, if any is being used, should be almost the last stage of programme-making. Televised news programmes, being produced to a tighter deadline, will have a more detailed preliminary script but it will not be finalised until the pictures are edited. If the pictures are cut to fit the words, the end result is either radio with pictures or an illustrated lantern show. This does not mean that nothing can be done before the editing and dubbing stages. There will often be a rough outline of the script before recording starts and, during

the course of the production, notes of phrases and sentences that could be used are made. Be careful here that you do not break the copyright laws: remember always to include the source of any material and whether you have quoted directly or summarised what another person has said or written. Scripts for studio-based productions are usually written in advance and a copy of the final version given to the teleprompt operator.

Writing words to pictures is a fine art. What the viewer is seeing and hearing must be connected: if they are not, it is the picture that is remembered rather than the words. The commentary must not simply describe what is being shown, it must add information that tells the audience more. Although what the viewer will see can be slightly anticipated, referring back won't work: the moment – and the picture – have passed.

Scripts for studio-based programmes present other considerations. A script here is usually concerned with conveying factual information, not creating a mood, reflecting an environment or representing a point of view, which a commentary might do. In a magazine programme or a news programme, items are generally introduced by a presenter or news-reader directly to camera. There may be cutaways to stills or clips of footage while the script continues. Hitting the right point in the script will be the responsibility of the director and vision mixer.

Although there will be small variations between the ways different companies and productions lay out their scripts and present information, the generally agreed conventions for a television studio script are:

1. What is seen appears on the left hand side of the page, what is heard on the right.
2. Visual sources, e.g. camera, VT, appear on the left, with cut lines indicating where they change marked in the script, while sound sources, e.g. grams, appear on the extreme right.
3. Information for the PA, director or vision mixer appear, often in a square, on the right. They will add the particular information they need by hand at the rehearsal.

CAM 1	PRESENTER:
MCU Presenter	Hello. In today's programme, we'll be talking to someone who says he can communicate
/PAN DOWN TO VEG/	with bees, looking at ways of cooking some of the exotic vegetables that are appearing in our supermarkets and getting an exclusive interview with the star of the film chosen for this year's Royal Command
VT 3	Performance./
Love Among the Ruins	
	In: 'Is this seat taken?...'
CAPGEN @ 5"	Out: '....and I never want to
Love Among the Ruins	see you again.'
Moonlight Productions	
	Dur: 30"
CAM 1	/PRESENTER: We'll find out later if that's how it ends. My
MCU Presenter	first guest is someone whose voice is more famous than her face. Nearly a quarter of us wake up to her Breakfast Show on radio but after ten years of getting up in the middle of the night, she's moving into television to present a series on
CAM 2	the changing role of women./
MCU LOUISE	Louise Fisher, why are you leaving radio?

Commentary scripts that are going to be pre-recorded need less information, but the spoken words still appear on the right hand side of the page. Timings are put in on the left.

| 0.05 | John has been a milkman since he left school ten years ago. He knew what he wanted to do as a small child. |

> 0.20   But now his job, and that of thousands of other milkmen, is under threat. Competition from supermarkets, the growth in the number of people living alone and new EC regulations may mean that the milkman will disappear from British streets.

Working with writers

In television or radio, the writer is usually someone involved in the preparation of the story: the producer, presenter or reporter. The writer of the script or commentary of a non-broadcast video, however, might not be involved until the later stages. The writer, at whatever stage he/she joins the production, may need notes of relevant research and to be briefed on the nature of the programme and the audience at which it is aimed, as well as copies of the visual material to be included. You may also need to brief the writer on any legal or ethical problems and supply sources of further information. If the writer is brought in later, the idea is not to direct him or her but to put yourself in the audience's position and to provide an outsider's response to the script. All suggestions for amendment need to be made with tact: the writer's job is to write and, as a breed, writers are no happier being told how to do their job than any other section of the population.

Check the script for factual accuracy, for any legal implications and for ambiguity. Does the context make it clear that two hundred pounds in weight or two hundred pounds in value is intended? It may be clear on the page, or after a moment's thought, but not when spoken.

Corporate videos and training tapes have additional considerations. Specialist writers are usually brought in and most expect to do their own research.

> Writing for corporate videos is not just a matter of craft skills. You also have to consider things like internal politics, confidentiality (which affects who you can ask for information or who you can show the script to) and knowledge which they take for granted but which is not at all obvious to an outsider. There is also the video's

shelf-life. It's not like in television where you have a definite transmission date. A corporate video will be around for two or three years so you have to consider what might change in that time. I was involved in working on a video for a clearing bank about induction into the company. In the end, the project was dropped because they kept reorganising the structure of the bank so it would have been out of date almost as soon as it was finished. Ultimately, the person commissioning the video is the one who must solve the problems but you need to know what problems might arise and, if possible, anticipate them. I was working on a video for a company where several departments all had an input and each one wanted the story told a different way. I didn't know which version the clients wanted to go with, so I had to call them for guidance. The client is the one with the final word.

Grant Eustace, freelance script writer

Writing – general principles

You may be asked to prepare or contribute to a draft script yourself. The considerations mentioned above will also apply but there are many other factors to consider when writing for a production.

Although a script or commentary is written, it is intended to be heard. Whatever the purpose, the idea is to produce something that sounds natural when spoken. Read it aloud. Does it sound the kind of thing you would say to explain what is going on to another person?

Language. The language used should be appropriate to the intended audience. Programmes that are aimed at a specialised sector can afford to use more slang or jargon but in general this is best avoided for two reasons: firstly, slang and jargon date, which will limit future sales, and secondly, the whole aim of jargon is to exclude those who are not members of a particular club, which will limit the audience.

Management-speak has come in for criticism because those who understand it despise its pompousness and those

who do not feel patronised. 'Downsizing the workforce' means a lot of people are going to lose their jobs. Medical jargon is regarded as a way of concealing the doctor's ignorance from patients: 'a non-specific infection of self-limiting duration' means 'I don't know what it is, but it'll clear up on its own'. Closer to home, you only have to listen to what is said on location or in the studio to realise that much film and broadcasting language is designed to blind the uninitiated with science.

Which brings up the matter of clichés. As the old joke has it, avoid clichés like the plague. Again, they date. Who now says 'sick as a parrot'? The person who invents a cliché is a genius, the next hundred people to use it are fools. If the phrase seems comfortingly familiar, ask yourself why. Sometimes news and current affairs programmes use clichés as a kind of shorthand: the viewer or listener understands in broad terms what is meant and that is probably enough for a news bulletin. Journalists are up against much shorter deadlines than other programme-makers so such short cuts are sometimes necessary.

Words of Anglo-Saxon origin have more power than those of Latin or Greek origin. This is why jargon is so often ineffective in putting across its message. Compare 'he was fired from the job he had held for twenty years' and 'his employment was terminated after two decades of service'. 'The child's mother said they did not know about the danger' might also be rendered 'The maternal parent of the infant declared neither was informed of the perilous circumstances'. Which of these examples has the greater sense of immediacy?

Verbs give impetus. Did someone run, jog, trot, escape, flee or bolt rather than go? Active verbs convey urgency and vigour so they should be used in preference to the passive tense, although this can be a useful technique to avoid pinning responsibility or blame on someone who might sue.

Are there any dangling participles (a phrase at the beginning of the sentence which does not refer to the subject of it)? For example, 'Getting into a taxi this week, the driver spotted my clerical attire…' (*Thought for the Day*, Radio 4, 1995). It was the cleric who was climbing into the taxi, not the driver. Sentences like this cause unease in the listener and will distract attention from what is being said for a moment.

Meaning. Classic FM used to run hourly forecasts introduced as '…the weather brought to you by Kuoni Travel'. This was wrong: it is God or meteorological forces that cause the weather. The travel company was bringing the weather <u>forecast</u>. Many listeners are intelligent enough to be so irritated by this that they miss the next few seconds.

The semantic distinction between uninterested, which originally meant not interested, and disinterested, meaning having no axe to grind, has now largely disappeared but there are other words which are often misused. A quantum leap can be very small, but significant, not necessarily very large and enough of the population has a scientific background to consider that anyone who makes this mistake is not to be trusted in other areas. King Canute knew that he couldn't hold back the waves; his demonstration was made in order to show up his courtiers' sycophancy. This is something that is regularly pointed out to journalists, with little noticeable effect. They go on writing and saying things like 'The Prime Minister, like Canute, has not been able to hold back the waves…'.

Juxtaposition. Many years ago Newham Council issued a leaflet. The title, *Racial Harassment – How You Can Help*, must have been discussed at countless meetings and have gone through several stages of drafting and proofing, yet no-one spotted the ambiguity produced by putting the two halves of the title side by side.

This happens more frequently when material is written in a hurry. 'The poet who survived the war with his family in Sarajevo…' was said on the *Today* programme in 1995. The context in this example made it clear that it was the civil war in former Yugoslavia to which the reporter referred, not a family feud. Although vocal inflections and timing may make it clearer what was intended, there is still a hiatus in which the listener mentally adjusts what was heard to what was meant.

Tautology. This is difficult to spot immediately but makes the script seem flabby. All school children are young, so saying 'a young schoolchild' is saying the same thing twice. Saying someone is a professional surgeon suggests comparison with an amateur surgeon, someone who carries out brain surgery in the kitchen as a hobby. Ask yourself, do they or would they come any other way?

Redundancy. This doesn't just occur when a company is downsizing. Some words are unnecessary. 'Appropriate measures will be taken.' Ask yourself, what would be the alternative? Inappropriate measures might indeed be taken but surely not intentionally. The word 'appropriate' is not necessary. This kind of flaccidity is very common in written statements from government departments or companies. If you are quoting a statement then what was said, however badly written, must be reported but there's no need to allow such verbal infelicities to appear in something over which you have some control.

Grammar. Among the audience will be people who were educated in the days when the rules of grammar were considered to be much less flexible than they are now. They form a large proportion of the writers of letters to the media. Some flinch at a split infinitive (an adverb between the two halves of a verb). 'To boldly go' grates on the ears of thousands throughout the country. *Star Trek* was an American series but higher standards are expected on this side of the Atlantic. Because of their nuisance value, self-styled experts on grammar can take up an irritating amount of your or someone else's time in replying to both letters and telephone calls. It's therefore simpler all round not to break the better known 'rules', unless the result is ugly, pretentious or does not put across the meaning as effectively.

These people are usually from the older section of the population. Different parts of the audience will contact the programme if the script says 'he' to refer to both men and women and if words that are deemed offensive are used for those from a particular ethnic origin or for someone with a specific physical or mental condition.

If someone says 'The Queen of England...' pained Scots will get in touch to point out that she is sovereign of Britain. Again, the hassle isn't worth it. There are some fine distinctions here: Great Britain refers to mainland England, Wales and Scotland, the United Kingdom consists of Great Britain and Northern Ireland. The adjective 'British', however, can refer to either.

The Colemanballs column in *Private Eye* will provide other examples of verbal infelicities, particularly extended metaphors. Most have been made live, but they do creep into programmes written and prepared under pressure.

Trade names

Trade names can be tricky. All of us now 'hoover' our rooms but that was originally the trade name of a particular type of vacuum cleaner. Many other trade names are used as a generic term – Biro, for example, should not be used as the general word for ballpoint pens. This is particularly important if you are, for example, comparing a number of similar objects for a consumer programme. You can't compare six types of Biro because a number of manufacturers make ballpoint pens. Your programme will almost certainly get a lawyer's letter, a complaint to the Broadcasting Complaints Commission and may have to make a public apology and pay damages if it criticises something erroneously described by a tradename when a rival manufacturer's product is under discussion.

Negative checks

This is the process by which a check is made to ensure that people or organisations are not unintentionally libelled. It mainly applies to drama – if the writer has created a crooked lawyer called Edwin Snodgrass who lives in a village called Little Piddling in the Marsh a check must be made, not only to see that there is no lawyer called Edwin Snodgrass but also that there is no lawyer of a similar name – say Edward Newgrass – living in a village of a similar name, like Little Puddleduck in the Marsh.

In current affairs or documentary programmes, it is worth checking that no organisation of a similar sounding name is operating in the same town, so that the script can be absolutely precise about which trading company is ripping the public off in one way or another.

Timing the script

A rough estimate can be made by calculating three words per second, but people vary in their speaking speed and the language and punctuation used may also affect the timing. Whoever is reading the script, if it is not the writer, may alter it to suit his/her own style, which could change the length or affect the way the words and the pictures interact. As it's not necessary to write over every shot and is indeed often more effective not to, the length of any silences have to

be timed accurately. Time the script by counting the words (some computer programmes will allow you to do this for scripts). If you read it yourself and use a stopwatch you will not get an accurate result, unless you are experienced in doing voice-overs.

Writing questions, intros and links

You may be asked to suggest questions for an interview. Although presenters usually prefer to use their own words, they must be clear why the question is being asked and what information is being elicited. You may also need to warn the presenter of potentially sensitive areas, either because they are to be avoided or because any questions need to be phrased carefully. Any legal issues must also be drawn to the presenter's attention.

Preparing questions for an interview on camera is different from getting ready for a research interview (see Chapter 2). When information is being gathered before the filming starts, interviews can be a more leisurely and discursive process because at this stage it will often not yet be known what is to be included and how the person is to be used. Questions are then designed to elicit as much material as possible so that particular opinions or experiences of the potential interviewee can be selected.

When recording or for a live transmission, however, briefer replies are needed, so closed questions are more often used, in order to get a concise answer. The research done before recording will have shown which replies the programme will need. You can suggest the kind of question to be asked on camera or you may be asking them yourself. Try to ask the question so that the contributor will answer with a complete sentence. This will make editing easier, especially if the questions are to be cut out.

Open questions are still useful but may be used to elicit a succinct reply by putting in more detail than at the preliminary research stage. For example, 'Tell me about the time when you…', 'Tell me what happened after you…', 'You have been widely quoted as saying…What is your opinion of this now?'.

Sometimes you will want a one-word answer, for example when doing a vox pop. The question to be asked should then be phrased to get a short reply. This usually means a

closed question, 'Do you think…?', 'Is the Prime Minister doing the right thing?', or similar wording.

The interview can be directed both by what is asked and how it is said. Interviewees will usually take the pace from the interviewer: if he/she is brisk and concise, so will they be. If the interviewer speaks quickly so will they. If the interviewer frowns and looks serious or smiles, so will they. This technique works both when recording for radio and when asking questions on camera.

Researchers may also be asked to write or draft an introduction for the presenter of a studio item or a link between one item and another. If it is to lead into a recorded insert, make sure that the last words of the introduction fit the opening of the insert, whether it is spoken or silent. Does the audience need any information to make sense of the item or to put it into context? It may need to be explained when an insert was recorded or why the place where it was done is important.

Presenter: Today, our reporter went to Brighton to see what effect rail privatisation is having on the tourist trade. She spoke to a hotelier there.

Insert: I haven't noticed much difference yet, but when summer comes…

If it's to introduce a guest, remember that the camera will cut to the guest when his or her name is mentioned. Your description of the guest's achievements should cover the areas of questioning in the interview or the audience's expectations will be raised but not satisfied. Unless there's a good reason not to, delay giving the name until very close to the end, or the camera will stay on the guest for an uncomfortably long time. You will also, of course, build up the suspense: who *is* this person?

Delaying information is a good tactic generally. Although the rule in programme-making is tell them what you're going to tell them, tell them and tell them what you've told them, this doesn't mean that everything has to be revealed immediately. How long you can delay the revelation depends on the audience – how keen will they be to find out, how long will they wait?

7
RECORDING THE PROGRAMME

By the time the programme comes to be recorded, either in the studio or on location, the bulk of the research should have been done. There may still be items to be checked but at this stage the researcher's role is one of monitoring what is happening to see if any new developments require changes to be made, reacting to circumstances and general dog's-bodying

so that the recording process goes ahead smoothly. On a live broadcast, however, or when collecting and setting up interviewees on the spot for, perhaps, a vox pop, the role is a more active one.

Looking after contributors

It is not enough to get contributors to turn up in the right place at the right time. They also have to be in the right frame to mind to give of their best, which includes being sober.

Contributors need to be well briefed about what is wanted from them so they feel confident, but not to the point of rehearsing their replies. Many will want to do this while equipment is being set up but they need to be tactfully steered away from it because the end result will be dull and flat. They may also find the process of being wired up with a microphone uncomfortable. Sound recordists are used to the process but contributors who are not should be informed what will happen. Where you can, introduce contributors to the crew, which will help them feel less uncomfortable and strange. As well as making them as much at their ease as possible, their safety must be considered. Think about:

- Equipment. The crew is used to taking action to avoid hazards; the contributors will not be. There are wires to trip over, pieces of equipment to avoid and, in the event of any emergency, they must be escorted to safety.
- Environment. On location weather conditions may have made the ground difficult to walk on; high winds may present problems and strong sunlight can dazzle.
- Action. What are contributors required to do? Will the demands of filming add hazards to carrying out an action, even if it is something they do all the time?

If you are working with someone who has any kind of problem, such as short-sightedness, deafness, mobility problems or an inability to read, even more care must be taken and potential dangers caused by their physical or mental condition anticipated.

Everyone warns against working with animals. This is sometimes unavoidable. There are legal regulations for the use of wild and domestic animals (see Appendix B). Although any animal hired in should have a competent handler, this

description cannot always be applied to pet owners. 'He's only playing...' is a phrase which often precedes a nasty situation. You may also find that other contributors on the show, especially children, are terrified of animals or birds.

Children bring other problems. They too must have a competent handler, either a parent or a chaperone, but their fascination with and curiosity about anything new, particularly equipment, needs to be borne in mind. Like pet owners, parents tend to be tolerant of their offspring's quirks, which can lead to accidents. There are stringent restrictions covering children who have to give a performance, depending on their age. You will need to get permission from parents or guardians even for documentary programmes. There are restrictions on what children may be asked to do and the number of hours they can work. See the section on the law for more information.

If there is any delay, or while the equipment is being set up, contributors who are not used to the media can become very tense. They may also disappear: worry has a significant effect on the bladder. On location, this is less of a problem as there are usually only a limited number of places where they might be, but large studio complexes offer a wider scope for getting lost. If the contributors require make-up, ensure both that the person responsible for summoning them to the studio knows where they are and that the make-up person knows at what time they will be needed.

Those who are used to appearing on the media present different problems. They may find delays annoying and even unflattering – surely no-one would prefer to extend another item when they are due to appear! The reasons for any wait need to be explained carefully and, if necessary, tactfully.

Briefing presenters

When working with reporters or presenters much will depend on the amount of involvement they have already had with the preparation. They may need to know:

- the background to the story;
- the structure of the programme and where the sequence they are recording fits in;
- the running order or schedule for the recording;
- why and how contributors they are interviewing are being used;

- any special information relating to contributors, including what not to ask.

Presenters and other members of the production team will also need to be informed of any changes that affect them, like alterations to the shooting schedule or to the running order.

Monitoring interviews

Once the contributor is in front of the camera, your responsibility is not finished. Although whoever is asking the questions will be aware of the content of the replies, he/she usually has other things to consider. A studio presenter may be getting instructions about timing, the next question to ask and other matters not directly concerned with the exact detail of what the interviewee is saying through an earpiece, as well as trying to talk to the guest. Under the pressure of appearing in front of the camera, it is easy for a contributor to make mistakes, either by getting a fact wrong or, more seriously, by contravening the law, perhaps expressing an opinion which might be construed as defamation.

The interviewer, too, is under pressure that might lead to slips, perhaps by omitting a vital question if the conversation strays off the main subject or getting a fact wrong, no matter how good the briefing. Although it is usually possible to correct mistakes during editing, it is obviously better to remedy any errors on the spot. If the programme is being transmitted live this is not possible so monitoring interviews is particularly important.

Having done the research, you are probably the most knowledgeable person about the subject of the interview so you may also be expected to come up with supplementary questions to make sure that everything to be covered is included.

When working on location with a single-camera crew, it may also be up to you to take note of the questions being asked so that, after the interviewee's answer has been recorded, reversal shots of the interviewer asking those questions can be shot, allowing the interview to be edited. This needs to be done accurately because the question must lead into the reply actually given. If there is a PA, this will usually be his/her responsibility.

Continuity

Continuity is the process of noting what happens in one shot so that there are no unexplained changes in the action or dress of the participants from one shot to another when the footage is edited together. For anything other than the simplest shoot, there should be someone to take continuity notes, either a production assistant or, for really complicated recordings, a continuity assistant. If there is not, you should be prepared to make notes that will ensure that the recording will edit together smoothly. Polaroid cameras are useful to back up notes and diagrams on:

- Dress. For example, on which lapel a brooch is being worn or on which side a shoulder bag or briefcase is being carried. If the filming is taking place over more than one day, the actual clothes being worn should be listed: men's ties and women's earrings can be a particular problem here. Contributors need to be asked to wear the same outfit on different filming days if necessary.
- Action. Which hand is a person using to hold an object or open a door? Are people walking left to right or right to left?
- The set. Where is the furniture, what is on a table or a mantelpiece? It is particularly important to record this if objects are going to be moved or you will be returning to the same place later on.

Checking captions, materials and sources

Before the recording starts, whether it is in the studio or on location, anything that has been obtained from a supplier must be checked against the order to ensure that it is what was requested, it is undamaged and in the right condition to be used. Where possible, this should be done well in advance but inevitably there will be situations when something has to be delivered on the day.

If you have a still or footage taken from a library of someone with a very common name, check that he/she does not share that name with another person in public life both when

ordering the material (see Chapter 4) and when it is delivered. Ensure that the script distinguishes between them, if necessary. There are two journalists called Duncan Campbell; two judges called John Baker (as well as a professor, a bishop and a judge Geoffrey Baker); three James Mitchells – a writer, an academic and a social security commissioner; the actor Anthony Hopkins and the composer Antony Hopkins. This last example also shows the need to check the spelling of people's names. Women's names, curiously, are less rarely duplicated but there's a model Kate Moss and a writer Kate Mosse.

- In the studio. The spelling of names and organisations must be correct and must be checked on the list of contributors given to the person preparing name captions. You should ensure that the list is in the right order. As the programme is going out, make sure that the name on the monitor indicating the next caption is correct. This is usually someone else's responsibility, but there's no harm in double-checking so long as you do it with tact.
- On a show using a number of VT inserts, it is usual for a member of the production team to be responsible for ensuring that they come up in the correct order and that any changes made in the running order are monitored and reported to the VT operators.
- On location. The director may want to do some simple rostrum camerawork on location, so check which pictures are needed. You will also need to ensure that any props or models have been delivered or will be taken to the location, whether it is you doing it or someone else in the production team.

8

POST-PRODUCTION

Editing

Because of the expense of hiring edit suites, the programme may be pre-edited off-line. This means keeping a master copy of the recorded footage, whether on film or video, and making a second copy on a cheaper, less high quality format. Both have time-codes. The cheaper version has this in vision and will be edited in an off-line suite, which has

fewer facilities and is less expensive than the on-line suite where the final version will be put together. Once the off-line edit has been done, a list of the time-codes on the shots used is made which can then be repeated, or conformed, using the master copy at an on-line edit. Any special effects are added at this point so notes of those needed must also be made during the off-line edit.

Editing can be done using either a linear or a non-linear system. Linear editing has, as the name suggests, to start at the beginning and go on to the end. This has disadvantages: it is impossible to change a sequence when reviewing the whole production at the end. The choices then are either:

1.   to use the existing tape as a source tape, cut out or add other material and go down a generation, which will involve loss of quality; or
2.   to relay the whole thing up to or after the section to be changed, which is time-consuming.

Non-linear editing restores the flexibility of film to video editing. The master version (either on film or video) of the production is transferred to a computer disc, again with time codes to ensure accurate matching. Because the material is on disc, it can be accessed in any order. It is also possible to store two or three versions of an edited sequence to decide which one to use. A list of time-codes is produced and the master version conformed. Non-linear editing systems can also do effects and these can be incorporated into the final list.

Apart from the material actually being edited, music and sound effects are the usual supplementary materials needed here. Captions are also put on at this stage, which means making sure that information to check they are accurate is brought to the edit.

The BBC's play on Albert Wintle in the series *Heroes and Villains*, transmitted in February 1995, used captions to indicate World War I locations. As many viewers called and wrote to point out, Ypres and Mons are not in France, as the captions stated, but Belgium. Several people must have been involved in producing the captions, yet no-one appeared to have checked the facts. Everything must be verified.

All the music needed must be brought along or delivered

to the edit suite or cutting room in the right format, whether it is on CD, vinyl disc or tape. This will involve checking in advance that the facilities to cope with any different formats are available or that transfer from one format to another is arranged.

Most edit suites or dubbing theatres have a full set of sound effects discs but, if it is a place you haven't used before, check. If a sound effect required is not on the standard discs, again ensure that it is delivered or taken there for the edit or dub in the right format. The duration of any sound dubbed on, whether music from a disc or an effect, must be recorded for clearance purposes, along with details of the disc from which it was taken.

Once the edit is finished, there will be documentation to be arranged. This will fall into the following categories.

- Technical information needed for transmission: the format of the final programme, length and nature of opening and end credit sequences, any extended periods of silence, unusual colour effects etc.
- Additional information that the commissioner might need for presentation announcements, such as the date when the programme was recorded, if this is significant, or what happened to major participants after recording. There may be other material, such as fact sheets or publications for sale connected to the programme. You must also consider what additional information about the programme needs to be passed to the company broadcasting it. Viewers telephone and write with queries of all kinds, from the address of an organisation mentioned to the background music used over a particular sequence. Names, addresses of organisations, locations, sources of any quoted material and music should be listed.

It is not just factual information that viewers want: if the programme contains potentially contentious material, the broadcasting company will also need to be alerted so they can take the decision whether to make an announcement before transmitting it. They may also have to prepare for their switchboards to be jammed, as the newspaper headlines will have it the next day.

Even if the production is not intended for broadcasting, there may be additional information that the client will need, which should be checked.

Billings and production information

You may also find yourself involved in the preparation of material for the press and public under the following headings:

- Billings. The information included in listings intended for the compilers of the programme pages in newspapers and periodicals must be prepared. The programme needs to be summed up in one or two sentences to sell it to the viewer, with a further paragraph or two which might be included, depending on the space available.

- Programme information. A summary of the programme's contents and, again, names and addresses of people and organisations should be supplied.

- Fact sheets. These need to contain a list of organisations included in the programme with, if necessary, fuller descriptions of the organisations' activities. Sometimes information about related organisations and material which was not used or a more detailed account of, for example, the laws relating to a particular issue will be added.

- Programme summaries and additional information for teletext pages.

- Books and pamphlets connected with the programme which are for sale. The material included is similar to that outlined above, as well as giving books consulted, stills (some of which may have to be specially supplied and cleared for inclusion) and graphic material.

- Notes for trainers or teachers relating to an educational production.

Publicity

Drawing attention to the programme is a vital part of the production process. After the programme is made, or even while it is being made, ways of publicising it have to be

considered. Sometimes a photographer might be hired to take publicity photographs for release to the press during the course of the production. What is to be included must be carefully considered: how much of the contents should be revealed, what problems are likely to arise, which contributors can be suggested to the press for back-up interviews and which will need to have their identity and privacy protected?

The broadcasting company will also have a department producing its own press material and will need information for publicity purposes. If the production is doing it itself, *Willings Press Guide* can be used to compile a list of newspapers (national and local) and periodicals (mass market, trade, hobby) intended to attract editorial coverage to whom you can send press releases. If the production is targeted to attract an audience with a particular interest, consider approaching specialist publications but find out their press dates: they may be put together up to a couple of months in advance, and allow for this when sending material or talking to the editorial staff. Given the sometimes long period between a journal going to press and the time it appears, this is not always an option.

All material released to the press and public has to be checked for factual accuracy, for any legal implications, including copyright, and for the effect on organisations and individuals it might create. There are occasions when people appearing in a programme must be protected from press attention.

If the production is expected to receive a lot of coverage, because of its subject matter, you might pass the names of people who are either in the programme or who were considered but not used to print journalists who will write articles. Anyone whose name is given must be told in advance and allowed to decide whether to co-operate. There's a fine balance to be struck between getting publicity and giving away so much information that the audience will think they've read all they need to know about the subject before the programme's transmission.

The broadcasting company might also want stills or clips to use in producing trails and making on-air announcements about forthcoming programmes. These need to be selected with equal care.

Preparing back-up material

Many programmes, particularly factual and educational ones, provide support material to viewers or teachers and the researcher may either have to provide information for its preparation or write it. This means keeping good records both of the programme's contents and of additional information that could be of use but which might not have been included in the programme. Some of this information might also be included on the teletext pages. Recipes are the most obvious example. If the programme is to be subtitled, a transcript should ideally be supplied (although this isn't always possible) and should be checked for accuracy, particularly in the spelling of names and organisations which might not be clear from the spoken word.

There may be a house style for support publications if the programme is to be part of a series. In this case, material must be prepared to match the layout and style. If, however, there is no set format, decisions about design, layout and writing style have to be agreed with both the member of the production team responsible and the publisher. As in every other area, time and budget will affect the final result. Although the publisher or printer will be ultimately responsible for the look of the printed material, the accuracy of the content is down to you, so drafts and the final copy must be meticulously proof-read.

APPENDIX A: COPYRIGHT

Copyright and other areas of the law are highly specialised areas which change, both because of new acts and also because of precedents set in test cases. The first modern copyright law was passed in 1911 but it has been modified by legislation in 1956, 1988 and 1995 and further amendments are due. The researcher cannot be expected to know the fine detail of these Acts but must be aware of their existence.

Copyright is an area in which whole armies of lawyers make a good and regular living. To adapt an old joke, two lawyers, three opinions. This section cannot turn you into an expert and you should not rely on it because it's necessarily over-simplified – there are exceptions to almost every principle cited here. Further problems arise with what is often referred to as 'layers of copyright'. You might want to include in your programme a clip of a poet reading from his/her work with a musical background. There may be copyright in the recording, in the poem and in the music to be cleared, as well as possible residual fees to the poet for the performance.

This section is just intended as a basic checklist to give an idea of when alarm bells should ring. The books listed in the reading list will give more information. If you know in advance the kind of problems you are likely to encounter, the more time you will have to check the position with an expert and set negotiations in motion.

What is copyright?

Copyright is a form of property, like a building. If you want to use it, you must come to an arrangement with the owner. It can be given as a gift or left in a will, sold outright to do what you want with or be loaned for a fixed time and under agreed conditions, i.e. you can rent all or part of the building and a certain sum of money may be charged for doing so. Conditions about what use you make of it may also be imposed – whether you can alter it in any way, for example.

This is how copyright works, except that what's owned is the work done, which is sometimes called intellectual property. This might be something written, or a painting, a photograph, a sculpture, a design, a musical composition or a piece of computer software. Rights may also be owned to a film, a tape, a translation of a literary work or the choreography of a ballet. Different rights (e.g. publication, theatrical) can be assigned or sold to different people or organisations. Rights can also be bequeathed in a will.

You cannot assume that if someone owns a work, that person also holds the copyright. The British Film Institute libraries, for example, contain both archive film and still pictures but they do not own the copyright to most of them.

There are associations, usually dealing with fine art or music, that will negotiate the rights to works done by their members and you should check whether the company or broadcaster you are working for has some arrangement with these organisations. This will save considerable time and effort but you still need to check if the person whose work you want to use is a member.

In general, employees of a company do not own the copyright in work they have done as part of their employment but this will depend on their contract of employment.

The copyright period

From 1 January 1996, copyright in a work in this country generally lasts until seventy years after the end of the year in which the creator of the work dies. Before that date the period was fifty years as it still is in some other countries. Thus, if an author or painter or photographer or whoever dies on 1 January, it is seventy years and 364 days (or 365 days in the case of a leap year) before his/her works enter the public domain in this country and the rest of the European Community.

This period of seventy years applies to all works, from something done while the originator was an infant prodigy of five to the last work published a few days before death. The sole exception to this is *Peter Pan* by J. M. Barrie (d. 1937). He gave the copyright in this work to Great Ormond Street Hospital, which will continue to be able to collect royalties on it, in whatever form it appears, for ever. His

other works, however, fall within the usual laws of copyright.

If the work is a collaboration, the copyright period extends until seventy years after the death of the longest-lived of the creators. Lennon and McCartney songs, for example, will come out of copyright after the songs that John Lennon wrote alone.

Because rights can be divided, you will almost certainly find that if your programme is to be sold abroad, some elements will have to be cleared again with the owner of the copyright in areas of the world to which you are selling it. This is particularly likely if your programme is a co-production and contains commercial music or film clips. You may also find that the period of copyright protection there is different.

If a production is to be sold on video instead of or as well as broadcast, those rights must be cleared with copyright holders too. The amount paid will depend on the size of the potential market, i.e. is it only likely to be sold to educational establishments or is it being aimed at a mass market?

Revived copyright arrangements

A work that was in copyright on 31 December 1995 will simply have its copyright period extended to seventy years. The mathematically or legally minded will realise, however, that the work of a number of authors, like Rudyard 'If' Kipling (d. 1936), or composers, like Sir Edgar 'Pomp and Circumstance March'[1] Elgar (d. 1934), whose copyright had lapsed, will now be back in the copyright period. Whoever owned the copyright before it expired is the owner of this revived copyright. Material which falls into this category can be used without permission but the copyright holder must be given notice and the terms for its use must be 'reasonable', which is where m'learned friend's services may be needed. Work commissioned before 1 July 1995 incorporating material that was then in the public domain but is now back in copyright, will be exempt. Proof, like a contract, will be required.

The Internet

At the end of 1996, 160 countries agreed treaties on copyright for certain types of work on the Internet. It is far too early to

---

[1] This is the tune to which 'Land of Hope and Glory' is sung. The words were written by A. C. Benson (d. 1925).

assess the implications for this for broadcasters but this is an area that production staff need to be aware of and to review regularly.

Work made available posthumously

A work found among an author's papers after his or her death, or discovered many years after, will be in copyright until fifty years after the end of the year in which it was first made available to the public or the year 2040, whichever is the sooner. There are six definitions of how a piece of work might be 'made available to the public'.

The publication right

This is a new area of copyright created by the most recent legislation. Usually copyright is owned by the author of a work but this gives rights to any person or organisation who makes available any piece of previously unpublished work in which copyright did exist, but has now expired. The period of copyright under this area lasts twenty-five years.

Parliamentary Copyright

Parliament (both Houses) owns the rights to work done by itself or under its control and copyright is administered either by the Speaker of the House of Commons or by the Clerk of the Parliaments. Parliamentary copyright lasts for fifty years from the end of the calendar year in which the work was made. Various provisions apply to the broadcasting of speeches made in Parliament.

Crown Copyright

This applies to work done by servants or employees of the Crown or government as part of their duties. It is a complex area, requiring expert knowledge, as copyright here may be for 125 years, seventy-five years or fifty years from the end of the calendar year of its making or publication. Note that Acts of Parliament become Crown Copyright once the Royal Assent has been received.

Anonymous and traditional works

Investigate very carefully if the work truly is anonymous – just because no-one in the office knows who did it doesn't mean it can't be discovered (think, for example, of an anonymous novel) and you will have to prove that you did all you could to find the copyright owner. Traditional is another area to be wary of – just because a song is being sung in a nasal whine by someone in open-toed sandals and an acrylic tank-top doesn't mean it's out of copyright.

Copyright does exist in anonymous or traditional works but here the important factor is when and how they were first made available to the public.

What can be copyright?

For the purposes of broadcasting and non-broadcast video, it's worth thinking of the kinds of copyright issues that might arise under four categories: words, pictures, sound and moral.

Words

Published words, whether prose or verse, may be subject to copyright. Are you quoting from a work still in copyright? Is what you're quoting a translation? This is a classic example of the kind of trap everyone has fallen into. When was the translation that you are planning to use made? The play you want to do may be a Greek tragedy written two thousand years ago but if you're using a translation (and most people would), is that in copyright?

Remember that songs consist of words (the lyric) as well as music. If you are using an opera whose libretto has been translated into English, is the translation in copyright? Hymns are a well-known trap here: old words or poems are often given new tunes and vice versa. *My Song is Love Unknown* was written in the seventeenth century but was almost unknown itself until given another tune by the composer John Ireland (d. 1962) when it became immensely popular with church congregations.

A book may be out of copyright, but a play or film adapted from it may not be. Works left uncompleted at

an author's death may be finished by another person: *The Mystery of Edwin Drood* by Charles Dickens is probably the best-known example.

Pictures

Still pictures. You need to find out who commissioned the work, i.e. was a photographer paid to do the work or was it done by a freelance? A photographer working for a company or a newspaper may not own the rights to the pictures he/she took: it will depend on what sort of contract he/she was working under.

Paintings, graphics etc. An organisation called the Design and Artists Copyright Society (DACS) will handle negotiations and payments to its members, but not all designers and artists belong to it.

Moving pictures. Most of the problems here arise not only from copyright clearances but also, especially in feature films and television drama productions, due to the contracts the performers, directors or writers originally signed. There will often be residual fees to be paid for repeats of television programmes. Post-1960 films may need clearance from actors, writers, the director and (if applicable) stunt men.

Productions made before the advent of home video will not have included these kinds of rights in the original contracts and your organisation may need to negotiate fees for their use with individuals, especially if you are working on a corporate or training video or one made only for the home video market.

News footage. This is protected by copyright until fifty years after the end of the year in which it was made.

Feature films. The situation in this case is more complicated. The copyright period here now lasts until seventy years after the end of the year in which the last of the following people dies:

1. the principal director of the film;
2. the writer of the screenplay;
3. the writer of the actual dialogue (who may be different from the writer of the screenplay);

4. the composer of music written for and used in the film.

As anyone who follows the Byzantine complications of the film world will know, there may be some difficulty in defining who is the 'principal' director or who 'the writer' is, especially where a number of people have worked on the screenplay and script.

The soundtrack of a film may involve two types of copyright: the film soundtrack itself which is treated as part of the film, so the owner of the film copyright will also own this right, and the sound recording copyright which could be sold to another party to exploit, e.g. by selling recordings of the soundtrack.

You may find that, even if your film is out of copyright, the owners of the print charge access fees. You may want to incorporate footage that was shot more than seventy years ago which was included in another programme and which can be obtained through a television company's library rather than the archive containing the original footage. Problems can occur here, because whether this can be done or not will depend on the contract agreed when the original production was made. There may have been a clause limiting the number of times it can be shown or even a clause requiring the film to be destroyed after use.

Sound

Music. This is a complicated area. Composers and song-writers usually sell copyright in their works to music publishers, who thus become the copyright owners. What is then done with the work becomes subject to other agreements.

There are two rights involved in broadcasting music: the right to record (i.e. to record music being played live on to tape or to copy a disc or tape in order to dub it on to a programme) and the right to broadcast music. The first is administered by the Mechanical Copyright Protection Society (MCPS), the second by the Performing Right Society (PRS).

A third organisation, Phonographic Performance Ltd (PPL), controls payments made for the use of already recorded music (i.e. commercial discs or tape) which is broadcast,

whether this is as part of a record programme on radio or because a commercial record has been dubbed on to a programme. For non-broadcast videos, the equivalent organisation is Video Performance Ltd (VPL).

You need to find out if the company for which you are working has any agreements with these organisations and what they are. If there is no agreement, you need to make one. The music business is very litigious and productions are monitored to find out whether broadcasters are complying with the law.

This is all very well when you can choose the music being played but on location it may be difficult to avoid music you have no control over – a football crowd singing, muzak in a hotel lobby, a ghetto-blaster on the shoulder of a passer-by. Ideally, of course, this kind of music wouldn't be in the programme, not because of copyright but because it can create editing problems. If it's unavoidable, however, the rules still apply and if what's being played is commercial music on disc or tape, it must still be cleared. If it's a crowd singing, you need to identify the song.

Because of the way the music industry is structured worldwide, different companies usually own the rights to a commercial disc in different parts of the world. Thus clearing a production containing commercial discs for sale around the world is complicated and expensive. Only the film world usually has the resources to do this.

Production music. Also called library or mood music, this is subject to copyright but can usually be cleared worldwide relatively simply without the complications involved in selling a programme containing commercially recorded music abroad.

Sound effects. These are, contrary to what some believe, copyright and need to be cleared like any other recorded sound. MCPS collects royalties on behalf of most, if not all, of the companies making production music and sound effects.

Theme music. The regulations attached to using a piece of music as the theme to a programme or series are different from those applied to music within a production.

Arrangements. The music you are dealing with may be out of copyright but the arrangement of it may have been done

only recently. If a brass band is playing the overture to *The Marriage of Figaro* (Mozart, d. 1791), you'll need to check if the arrangement for brass band as opposed to a full orchestra is in copyright. Folk music is another area where, although the song may be trad or anon, the arrangement may have been done last week and may constitute a copyright element. *The House of the Rising Sun* is a folk song which became a hit for the Animals in 1968 and, as something of a classic, has been regularly played ever since. A member of the group has said that they all collaborated on the arrangement but only the name of Alan Price appeared as the arranger so only he receives royalty payments for that version. At least two other recordings, by Joan Baez and Nina Simone, have also been made.

Unfinished works. It is not only Schubert who left symphonies unfinished. Many composers, especially in earlier periods, wrote down only the tune, leaving harmonies and orchestrations unrecorded. Modern editors may have completed a work you wish to use.

The spoken word. Copyright in the spoken word was clarified by the 1988 Act. Since then the spoken word, as in an unscripted interview, is subject to copyright law. Only if the contribution is a literary work, however, does this apply. Thus, if you are doorstepping a villain who invites you to 'Naff off', it is unlikely this would be deemed to have any literary merit. But don't rely on your own definition of what constitutes potential GCSE fodder in a less clear-cut case – talk to an expert.

You can save a lot of hassle with people wanting to withdraw an interview they gave you by getting them to sign a contract on the spot – this is worth doing even for vox pops – that gives your organisation the rights to their contribution. If they become famous or notorious later, you've got a nice little earner and even if they don't you can wave it at them if they have second thoughts.

Moral rights
This area was created by the 1988 Act so the law may be different for works created before and after 1 August 1989.

Paternity. This is the right to be identified as the author of a work and has to be claimed in writing. When you sit through the credits of a recent film you usually see the paternity right claimed in some form of words and books now usually have a paragraph detailing who is legally the author. Broadcasters must in general identify the author clearly and prominently. It's worth noting that the paternity right may have been claimed in a way, for example a contract, which is not obvious to a researcher, or may have been waived.

Integrity. This is the right not to have work subjected to derogatory treatment, i.e. it must not be edited or altered in any way that makes the author look stupid. With recorded interviews, there is some overlap with copyright in the spoken word. Get advice.

Privacy. This is nothing to do with the invasion of privacy. It's the right not to have pictures and videos commissioned for private and domestic use used without permission. The aim is to prevent people selling copies of work they were commissioned to do without the knowledge of the subjects.

Burlesques and parodies

If you want to use a parody of a work, you may have to get the original author's permission. Whether you need permission or not depends on how 'substantial' a part of the original work you are using. It's unwise to rely on a parodist's assurance that it is being done with consent – especially if the parodist is busking outside a pub. In the case of a song, of course, the music constitutes a separate copyright element and will have to be cleared in any case.

Major exceptions

Use of an insubstantial part. Using an 'insubstantial' part of a work is as much a question of quality as quantity. The rule-of-thumb is generally, and mistakenly, taken to be ten per cent, but what is ten per cent of a four-line poem? You may only show a thirty second clip of a movie but if it's the pivotal thirty seconds when the villain is unmasked, that would not be regarded as insubstantial.

Fair dealing. There are various conditions under which a copyright holder's permission does not need to be obtained before using his/her work. In all cases, only enough of the work to make the point can be used: whether the amount used is 'fair' is a matter for experts or the courts to decide.

- Research or private study. This covers things like copying material, such as extracts from a book or academic article, for the purpose of researching a production.
- Reporting current events. This does not, however, cover photographs.
- Review or criticism of a work. This does not include biographical or general use and where one blends into the other is a matter of expert legal opinion.

Penalties

Sometimes, no matter what research is carried out, it is impossible to clear copyright on every element in a programme. Efforts to find the copyright holder need to be well documented. In general, a copyright holder is entitled only to recover the sum of money that would have been paid if something is used without permission, but to that potential sum must be added the costs of any legal action. The copyright holder may also get an injunction to prevent the production being transmitted or distributed.

Where there is no clear precedent, estimates of the cost of transgressing the law are hard to make. Any decision whether to do an expensive re-edit or to cross the fingers, transmit and wait for the lawyer's letter needs to be made by someone in authority who will take the responsibility for that decision. Bear in mind, however, that copyright infringement is a criminal offence which can be punished with imprisonment and you will not be popular if you get your employer locked up!

Is it copyright?

Some fees due to various people whose work you want to use are not, strictly speaking, to do with copyright. If you want to show an excerpt from a film or television play, certain

people – actors, directors, stunt arrangers etc. – may be due residual payments for repeats, as agreed in the contract they signed with the company that made the film. These will vary from production to production and original contracts have to be checked. However, performers' rights under the Copyright Act often parallel the copyright provisions.

You may also find that if you're filming a band or a group, the musicians will ask for payment: this is not to do with copyright but to do with Musicians Union agreements and you will almost certainly still have to pay the owner of the copyright to the music played.

You may pay an art gallery a fee to film in it. This does not cover filming the exhibits: the gallery is unlikely to own the copyright of the works. What you have paid is a facility fee: copyright still has to be negotiated with the artist or sculptor or the owner of the rights, if you are featuring the works. If you use a transparency of a work of art owned by a gallery, you will probably have to pay a reproduction fee, even if the work itself is long out of copyright, because the photograph made of the work is itself copyright.

APPENDIX B: THE LAW AND ETHICS

Many lawyers spend their working lives arguing whether a casual remark is or is not defamatory or whether an action was done maliciously. The ramifications of the law are too complex for people doing research to rely solely on their own knowledge and judgement. It is one thing to know the wording of an Act, but another to know how it has been, or will be, interpreted thus establishing a precedent in law. Some aspects of the law have not yet been tested in the courts. The reading list gives books containing much more detail than can be included here. This section gives only an indication of potential problems and a very limited summary of the complex laws that surround these subjects. Get advice because this is, like copyright, an area where a little knowledge is a dangerous thing.

> *What the Papers Say* (Granada Television) used to be written on Thursday and recorded on Friday. Because it was on current affairs and presented by journalists, who can be critical, it had to be checked by the company's lawyers. I took the script to them on Thursday and first thing on Friday phoned them up. They'd noted anything they thought might cause problems, which I might argue about with them, but in the end, we were paying them for their expertise so went with what they said. I then had to persuade the journalist presenting the edition to change the script. If there's any legal action, it's the broadcaster's responsibility: they get sued not just the presenter.
>
> *Stephen Kelly, ex-Granada researcher*

The laws that are likely to affect people working in the media here divide into three broad areas which will be considered in the following few pages.

Dealing with the government

Election law. Under the Representation of the People Act of 1983, legislation applies to the broadcasting and reporting of elections. This period begins, in the case of a General Election, when the date Parliament is to be dissolved is announced or when the Queen announces that she intends to dissolve Parliament. For by-elections, this starts with the issue of the writ. There are also regulations covering elections to the European Parliament.

Official secrets. The government can classify anything, even down to the menu in a Civil Service canteen, as an official secret, but there are six major categories relating to defence and national security. The Defence Press and Broadcasting Advisory Committee only offers 'guidance' not legal restrictions. Defence advisory notices are sent to newspaper editors and television companies but, if you're working for an independent company that does not receive them, they can easily be obtained.

Sedition. This is defined as 'words which are likely to disturb the internal peace and government of a country'.

Reporting Parliamentary proceedings. There is some overlap here with the laws on copyright and defamation. Recordings of proceedings can be used mainly for news and current affairs or educational programmes. Clips in light entertainment or magazine programmes must be used with caution and expert advice.

Reporting legal proceedings

Juveniles. (A child is under fourteen, a young person over fourteen but under eighteen.) Unless reporting restrictions are lifted by the Court or the Home Secretary, the names or any information (like parents' names or addresses, schools etc.) that might identify a juvenile involved in any legal process (including tribunals, custody and wardship cases) may not be disclosed.

Contempt of court and intention to commit contempt of court. These terms cover anything that might prejudice the outcome of a trial.

Appeals. Someone who was convicted of an offence may later be cleared on appeal and this needs to be checked. Appeals either against the verdict or the length of the sentence sometimes take place a long while after the original trial and may not receive a great deal of publicity so you need to be careful about this.

Inquiries. Although public inquiries are usually held in public, the Secretary of State can direct that evidence considered contrary to the national interest should not be reported.

Rehabilitation of Offenders Act 1974. Convictions are regarded as spent, and should not therefore be referred to, after a specified length of time, which varies according to the severity of the sentence, not the crime.

Sexual offences. Victims of various sexual offences are granted anonymity but for some offences this applies to females only, e.g. intercourse with a girl under thirteen or one aged between thirteen and sixteen. This restriction can, in certain circumstances, be lifted by a magistrate or a judge and a woman who is raped may also agree to be identified.

Civil actions. A judge may, or sometimes must, hear some civil actions 'in chambers', i.e. in private. Reporting what happened there may constitute contempt of court.

Bankruptcy, company liquidation, tribunals and inquests. These are all legal proceedings to which various restrictions apply.

Individuals

Defamation, libel and malicious falsehood. The first two are something that would 'tend to lower the plaintiff in the estimation of a right thinking member of society' and, like many legal definitions, begs more questions than it answers. The third is something that might damage the person named, even if it doesn't criticise him or her. There are defences: is what was said true and can it be proved, or is it fair comment, not done maliciously, factually based and on a matter of public interest?

Some areas of public life, such as statements in Parliament, in courts and other legal proceedings, like tribunals,

and in government documents are considered privileged. Those making them are protected from legal action but only in those circumstances. An MP may risk proceedings if he/she repeats outside the House of Commons a statement already made inside. The media has only qualified privilege when reporting, which means that there must be some public interest and that the report was neither inaccurate nor made maliciously.

Breach of confidence. This applies to information given in confidence. This might not be directly given to a researcher or journalist by the person to whom it relates: it might come through someone who was told something in confidence or from a person, e.g. an employee of a company, whose contract of employment has a confidentiality clause, either written or implicit. Some people, like doctors or priests, have a professional obligation not to repeat things told to them. This is also a potential growth area for those who feel their privacy has been invaded. They may claim that information about them was obtained in circumstances of confidentiality.

Race relations. Under the Public Order Act (1986), care needs to be taken when reporting what someone said if it is likely to stir up hatred against any racial group. Even though it may be made plain that what was said is illegal, the act of repeating it might be illegal. This also applies to defamation: reporting a defamatory statement made by someone else may lead to legal action.

Using children in productions

A number of items of legislation cover the use of children in productions. The regulations largely apply to productions where children are giving a performance, but if you are working on a documentary involving children for long periods, you need to ensure you do not transgress the laws.

There are limits to the hours, including rehearsals, that children may work and they must have a responsible adult, a parent or a chaperone, with them. If they are to be used over a long period, rest periods and educational facilities may have to be provided. They must have their parents' or guardian's permission to appear and may also need permission from their headteacher or local authority. Schoolchildren need to

Table B.1 Working with children[1]

Age (years)	Maximum hours on location/in studio	Permitted times of day on site	Maximum length of continuous performance	Maximum length of total hours of performance or rehearsal
Under 2	3	0930–1600	20 min	1
2–5	5	0930–1630	30 min	2
5–9	7½	0900–1630	45 min	3
10–12	7½	0900–1700	45 min	3
13–16	8	0900–1900 or 1000–2200[2]	1 hr	3½

[1] A child is legally defined as someone who is under the school leaving age. Employing children as performers is covered by the Children (Performances) Regulations 1968. There are also minimum intervals for meals and rest. There are restrictions on the type of performances children under fourteen may give and they must be licensed by the Chief Magistrate at Bow Street Court, 192 Bow Street, London WC2 7AS. All children under the age of eighteen must be licensed to perform outside the United Kingdom and the Irish Republic.

[2] This only applies to studio performances, and a licence must be obtained.

be licensed to perform if they will be working more than four days in six months (see Table B.1). It's worthwhile building up good relations with your local LEA contact.

There are other restrictions applying to children. Under sixteen they can't take part in any potentially dangerous performance. Between twelve and sixteen, they need a licence to be trained for any potentially dangerous activity and under twelve they cannot even be trained for this. A child under thirteen cannot drive any farm vehicle, including tractors. Regulatory body standards and codes of practice impose other limits. Children should not, for example, be exposed to any kind of distress which can apply to both a part they might be playing in a drama or questions put to them in a news or documentary programme.

Identical twins are much in demand where performances involve long shooting hours. You get twice as many hours because, although their mother will be able to tell them apart, the average viewer cannot tell which twin is appearing in which scene.

Working with animals

It's not just because of their unpredictable behaviour that people are warned against working with our furred and feathered friends. There are four main Acts that apply to the use of animals when filming in this country, although the law abroad and even in Scotland or Northern Ireland may be different:

1.   The Protection of Animals Act (1911) which basically legislates against the ill-treatment of animals.
2.   The Performing Animals (Regulation) Act 1925. Under this, people must have a licence, issued by the local authority, to exhibit or train performing animals, as in a circus. The exceptions are the police, military, agricultural establishments or those doing so for sporting purposes. This may be relevant to a production wanting to use trained animals.
3.   The Cinematograph Films (Animals) Act (1937) prevents the showing of any film where cruelty to animals was involved in its making. Under the provisions of this Act, even if you are making a programme about a cruel and illegal practice, such as badger-baiting, you may not be able to record or show what happens.
4.   The Dangerous Wild Animals Act 1976 which requires anyone keeping a wild animal privately to have a licence. Circuses, zoos, pet shops and certain scientific laboratories are excluded. There is a very long list of species which are, for the purposes of the Act, defined as wild; everything from aardvarks to wolverines, via cassowaries, okapi and pronghorns. You may also need an encyclopaedia of wildlife to find out if the exotic pet being kept in a block of flats is legally entitled to be there.

Different regulations apply to domestic animals. The Animal Health section of the local Ministry of Agriculture, Fisheries and Food (MAFF) branch can give advice and, on occasions, will need to know what you are doing with farm animals. Wild, endangered and protected species are the province of the Department of the Environment. If you want to bring an animal into the country to film it, Customs and Excise also become involved.

Getting animals to locations can present problems. Under the Pig (Records, Identification and Movement) Order 1995, anyone who owns a pig must register it with the local branch of MAFF and, if it needs to be moved, obtain a licence to do so if this is not to be from one farm to another. This Order includes wild boar. You may also not feed a pig with household scraps, no matter how hungry it seems nor how sorry you feel for it. Sheep and cattle must also be accompanied by a Movement Declaration Order stating where the animal is coming from and where it is going to. The local Animal Health Office will again advise.

Restrictions on transporting animals in parts of the country apply when there are outbreaks of particular, virulent diseases, like foot and mouth disease, swine fever or rabies. Check with the local branch of MAFF.

The RSPCA has issued guidelines about working with animals. Most are concerned with using animals in drama productions but there is also good advice about dealing with animals generally. Above all patience and consideration for the animal's welfare, not just the avoidance of cruelty, are required. A tired, unhappy or unwell animal will not only come across badly but may also be dangerous to performers, contributors and crew. It is always a good idea to find out the telephone number and address of a local vet when recording on a location where animals are to be used and to know where the nearest doctor or hospital with an accident and emergency department is. Any injury at all, whether to animals or humans, should be treated immediately.

Miscellaneous Acts

As well as the laws relating to the government, legal proceedings and individuals, either human or animal, there are four others which need to be taken into account. The first two affect what can be shown, the third, how research information can be stored and the last concerns the access police may have to research material.

Blasphemy. This can only be against the tenets of Christianity. The Christian churches themselves seem disinclined to pursue productions that might be thought blasphemous but, because the law remains on the statute books, individuals can still bring private prosecutions. As Salman Rushdie's

experiences show, even if other faiths cannot call in the law to protect them against blasphemy, they can still create trouble for you and your company.

Obscenity. What is regarded as obscene is a matter of prevailing morality. What is considered perfectly acceptable, even normal, in one section of society may be thought totally depraved and corrupt in another. This is another area where there are a great number of statutory provisions.

The Data Protection Act. This Act requires that if information about individuals is held on computer, the computer must be licensed and people given access to what is held on them. This is why many people still prefer to use notebooks, index cards and other less technologically advanced forms of keeping records.

The Police and Criminal Evidence Act (1984). Known as PACE, this Act allows the police to obtain journalistic material, including video tapes, to use in evidence where a serious arrestable offence has been committed. A judge must approve an order and the police must give notice that they are applying for an order before the material is surrendered.

Ethics

What is an ethical consideration here can be legally enforceable elsewhere in the world, so aspects of the law overseas must be taken into account if you are working on a co-production or hoping for overseas sales. American laws on the invasion of privacy, for example, are very stringent. In France, you can defame the dead.

In most situations, the people you deal with need to trust you and this starts with how you represent yourself to them. Anyone can call themselves a producer. There's nothing wrong with promoting yourself slightly from researcher to assistant producer or whatever if you are dealing with someone to whom status matters but you should not directly lie about your production's status: if you have not yet been commissioned by a broadcaster don't say that you are doing something for Channel 4 or for the BBC. This can be a matter of careful wording: you can say you're gathering material for a programme to be submitted to a company, for example.

None of this applies to investigative reporting where you may find yourself pretending to be an ordinary punter in order to expose wrongdoing. This area is a whole can of legal and ethical worms. The broadcaster for which you are working may have guidelines on ringing up or writing, quite apart from legal considerations, which may also apply. If you're working for a small independent, there may be no company policy but the final purchaser of the programme may be constrained by regulations or codes of practice on broadcasting information obtained in an undercover manner, including taping telephone calls and surreptitious filming. This is where you need a book on the law as it applies to the media, a copy of broadcasting codes of practice and access to a good lawyer.

Your next responsibility is to the contributors. Very few people who have not encountered it have much idea of the impact appearing in the media can have on their lives. You need to take this into account for them. Could their co-operation lead to criminal prosecution, for example? The production can also get into very tricky legal waters when dealing with criminals.

Less dramatically, what are their family, friends and neighbours likely to feel and do? How will what they say affect their job prospects, either now or in the future? These have to be balanced against the public good and the right to know, but as a general rule, people should be allowed to make an informed decision about whether to participate.

On a *Late Show* special about the mood-altering drug Prozac, we were trying to prove or disprove Freud's theory that artistic or creative people tend to be depressive. I had to find half-a-dozen depressive, creative types and persuade them to take Prozac for six months.

I read all the bumph about Prozac and books and articles about creative people to find people to take part. The hard part was persuading them to do it. Some I approached denied that they were depressive – they got all their angst out of their system by writing about it. It took about two months to set up. I got to know them and had to gain their trust by a combination of

charm and reasoning, talking through the pros and cons. One or two agreed, then got cold feet and dropped out just before it started but I had lined up eight or ten and in the end we filmed six – writers, a painter, a poet and a couple of musicians. One of the writers dropped out while we were filming partly for personal reasons and partly because the Prozac had the opposite effect from what it was intended to do, it made her depressed.

Talking it through and getting the people's agreement was only half the work. I had to be responsible about it. The film had to satisfy the BBC's editorial criteria and it was cleared at a high level. We also had to get them to sign a disclaimer without frightening them off. A clinical psychologist was directing it and provided expert back-up and reassurance. They also had to be seen by a GP, because the drug can only be prescribed by a qualified doctor, and I had to get the consent of their own GPs, but none refused.

Geoff Prout, freelance assistant producer

You also need to consider how true a representation of the interviewee the material you gather is. In television, where there is usually time between the initial contact and the recording of an interview, people have time to reconsider their position but in radio, where most interviews are simply taped on the spot, this is a serious matter. All sorts of outside events can influence what a person says: a difficult journey to work may have put the interviewee in a bad mood so that what is said is more emphatic and severe than the situation warrants.

There are other ethical considerations relating to contributors. It is a maxim that sources should always be protected. This is not solely a matter of altruism. If you become known as a person who betrays sources, people will be less willing to help you in the future. Although this goes against the grain, you may have to destroy papers and other information received where these might identify who sent them. Although certain types of journalistic material are excluded from the Police and Criminal Evidence Act, the

police have powers to obtain an order to take material in defined circumstances. These could reveal sources.

Under the Broadcasting Act (1990), various areas are controlled in broadcast programmes. They are:

- violence;
- breaches of good taste and decency;
- encouragement or incitement to crime;
- anything that might lead to public disorder;
- anything offensive to public feeling.

These are not defined in law but are covered in the broadcasters' codes of practice. There is a 9 p.m. watershed: material shown after that time can be more powerful, on the assumption that children will not be watching.

There are a whole host of other areas of sensitivity which need to be considered. The broadcasters have detailed guidelines on, for example, 'bad' language, which is an area that viewers are very exercised about.

The ITC issues a Code of Programme Sponsorship defining how and in what circumstances programmes or parts of programmes can have production costs met, either in whole or part, by an organisation not involved in programme-making in order to promote itself. The BBC also has guidelines covering co-productions and co-funding.

> I wouldn't pursue an idea if a company who agreed to sponsor our films wanted too much control or product placement. I won't compromise the good name of the hospital or the medical school. Although I'm in the business of cost recovery, I'm also here to raise the hospital's profile nationally.
>
> *David Cleverly, Producer Video Unit*
> *St George's NHS Healthcare Trust and Medical School*

FURTHER READING

Chapter 1: The production process

There are a number of books covering communication skills and working as part of a team which will be in the local library or bookshop. It is important for all members of the production team to understand the roles and responsibilities of their colleagues. On a small, independent production researchers may have to do some of the work traditionally done by production managers or production assistants. The following books contain useful information on all aspects of production so will also provide further information for other chapters:

Crisp, Mike *The Practical Director* (Focal Press)
Croton, Gordon *From Script to Screen* (BBC Television Training)
Fraser, Cathie *The Production Assistant's Survival Guide* (BBC Television Training)
Freeman, Diane *The Production Handbook* (PACT)
Gates, Richard *Production Management for Film and Video* (Focal Press)
McLeish, Robert *Radio Production* (Focal Press)
Millerson, Gerald *Effective TV Production* (Focal Press)
Rowlands, Avril *The Television PA's Handbook* (Focal Press)

Chapter 2: Developing, researching and presenting ideas

Most trade associations produce a yearbook or a list of members which you should be able to find in the reference section of a large library. You will also find there encyclopaedias, the Guinness Book of Records, books of quotations, biographical dictionaries, maps etc.

Chater, Kathy *The Television Researcher's Guide* (BBC Television Training) – contains addresses and telephone numbers of useful organisations in all fields.
Directory of British Associations

Family Welfare Association *Charities Digest*

Fisher, Ron *A Schindler Survivor: The Story Behind the Documentary* – available, while stocks last, from Carlton Television, PO Box 1, London W14 8UB.

Fisher, Paul and Peak, Steve *The Media Guide* (Fourth Estate)

Hollis Press and Public Relations Annual (DPA)

Millard, Patricia (ed.) *Trade Associations and Professional Bodies of the United Kingdom* (Gale Research International)

Viljoen, Dorothy *The Art of the Deal* (PACT) – this covers the business aspects of production making, including sources of finance, production agreements, contracts and rights. Although aimed at those involved in production management, it gives details of the type of information commissioners need so is useful when developing and selling ideas.

Chapter 3: Selecting and working with contributors

Contributors will mainly come from the organisations mentioned in the previous chapter's booklist. There are also books on the interpersonal and communication skills needed to conduct successful interviews. Browse through the ones in the local library or bookshop to find the one that seems to suit your particular needs.

Chapter 4: Acquiring and using visual and audio material

Ballantyne, James (ed.) *Researcher's Guide to British Film and Television Collections* (British Universities Film and Video Council)

Ballantyne, James (ed.) *Researcher's Guide to British Newsreels* (British Universities Film and Video Council)

Cambridge Guide to the Museums of Britain and Ireland (CUP)

Evans, Hilary and Mary Evans (ed.) *The Picture Researcher's Handbook* (Routledge)

Hudson, Kenneth and Nicholls, Anne *Directory of Museums and Living Displays* (Stockton Press)

Montagu, Ralph *Graphics* (BBC Television Training)

Pank, Bob (ed.) *The Digital Fact Book* (Quantel) – contains slightly more than a researcher needs to know about technical standards.

Weerasinghe, Lali *Directory of Recorded Sound Sources in the UK* (British Library)

Addresses

BAPLA (British Association of Picture Libraries and Agencies), 13 Woodberry Crescent, London N10 1PJ (Tel. 0181-883 2531)

FOCAL (Federation of Commercial Audio Visual Libraries Ltd), PO Box 422, Harrow, Middlesex HA1 3YN (Tel. 0181-423 5853) – is the UK-based international organisation for audio-visual libraries and the professional film researchers who access them. Their members' guide gives a list of all members and what footage, in general terms, the libraries hold and what the researchers have worked on if you need a specialist film researcher.

Moving Image Society – BKSTS, 63–71 Victoria House, Vernon Place, London WC1B 4DJ (Tel. 0171-242 8400) produces a series of wallcharts on film and video formats.

Chapter 5: Assessing and recommending locations and studios

If you are involved in selecting facilities and studios, you can assemble a free collection of material about many of those available from various trade fairs and conferences where companies and organisations, including regional film commissions, exhibit. There are a number of directories of facilities and services, some on CD-ROM, including:

The Broadcast Production Guide (International Thomson)
Direct (MDI)
The Knowledge (Miller Freeman Information Services)

Other publications giving information, in addition to those listed under Chapter 1, about recording in studios and on location include:

Champness, Peter *Camera Mountings* (BBC Television Training)
Jarvis, Peter *Shooting on Location* (BBC Television Training)
Jarvis, Peter *The Essential Director's Handbook* (Focal Press)
Jarvis, Peter *The Essential Television Handbook* (Focal Press)
Phillips, Brian *Stand By, Studio!* (BBC Television Training)
Talbot-Smith, Michael *Sound Assistance* (Focal Press)

The Health and Safety Executive produces publications on safety, including one written by the Broadcasting and Related Industries Joint Advisory Committee aimed at freelancers.

Chapter 6: The script

The Economist's *Style Guide*, although intended for print journalism, is also valuable in broadcasting. As well as guidance on writing, there is a reference section including such things as capital cities, the names of currencies used in countries and differences between words used in America and Britain, which is useful if you are working on a co-production.

Bryson, Bill *Troublesome Words* (Penguin)
Eustace, Grant *Writing for Corporate Video* (Focal Press)
Mansfield, John *Narration and Editing* (BBC Television Training)

Chapter 7: Recording the programme

Dinsdale, Stephen *A Quick Crib to Television Stage Management* (BBC Television Training) – although this covers drama production, many of the topics covered are relevant to documentaries and entertainment programmes.
Rowlands, Avril *The Continuity Handbook* (Focal Press, 1994)
Singleton-Turner, Roger *Continuity Notes* (BBC Television Training)

Chapter 8: Post-production

Lyver, Des and Swainson, Graham *Basics of Video Production* (Focal Press, 1995)

Appendix A: Copyright

Crone, Tom *Law and the Media* (Focal Press, 1995)

Edwards, Stephen *Rights Clearances for Film and Television Productions* (PACT)

Flint, Michael F. *A User's Guide to Copyright* (Butterworths, 1990)

Greenwood, Walter and Welsh, Tom *McNae's Essential Law for Journalists* (Butterworths)

Miller, Phil *Media Law for Producers* (Focal Press)

Addresses

DACS (Design and Artists Copyright Society Ltd), Parchment House, Northburgh Street, London EC1 (Tel. 0171-336 8811)

MCPS (Mechanical Copyright Protection Society), Elgar House, 41 Streatham High Road, London SW16 1ER (Tel. 0181- 769 4400)

PRS (Performing Right Society), 29–33 Berners Street, London W1P 4AA (Tel. 0171-580 5544)

PPL (Phonographic Performance Ltd), Ganton House, 14–22 Ganton Street, London W1V 1LB (Tel. 0171-437 0311)

VPL (Video Performances Ltd) – administers rights in music videos for its members; it operates from the same address as PPL.

Appendix B: The law and ethics

BBC *Guidelines for Factual Programmes* (BBC)

Crone, Tom *Law and the Media* (Focal Press, 1995)

Greenwood, Walter and Welsh, Tom *McNae's Essential Law for Journalists* (Butterworths)

Addresses

The Secretary, DPBAC, Room 2235, Ministry of Defence Main Building, Whitehall, London SW1A 2HB (Tel. 0171-218 2206)

Channel 4, 124 Horseferry Road, London SW1P 2TX –

Independent Television Commission (ITC), 33 Foley Street, London W1P 7LB (Tel. 0171-255 3000) – produces codes of practice for ITV programme-makers.

INDEX